S*The*TAMP
of AUSTRALIA

For Leni

The STAMP *of* AUSTRALIA

The story of our mail—from Second Fleet to
twenty-first century

KELLY BURKE

ALLEN&UNWIN

First published in 2009

Original concept for *The Stamp of Australia*: Hammerklavier Productions.

Allen & Unwin
83 Alexander Street
Crows Nest NSW 2065
Australia
Phone: (61 2) 8425 0100
Fax: (61 2) 9906 2218
Email: info@allenandunwin.com
Web: www.allenandunwin.com

National Library of Australia
Cataloguing-in-Publication entry:

Burke, Kelly.
    The stamp of Australia : the story of our mail – from Second Fleet to
    twenty-first century / Kelly Burke.

    ISBN: 9781741756456 (hbk.)
    9781741756449 (pbk.)
    9781741756142 (pbk.)

    Includes index.

    Australia Post—History.
    Postal service—Australia—History.
    Australia—History.

383.4994

Index by Trevor Matthews
Internal design by Nada Backovic
Set in 12.5/16 pt Goudy Old Style by Midland Typesetters, Australia
Printed in Australia by McPherson's Printing Group

10 9 8 7 6 5 4 3 2 1

CONTENTS

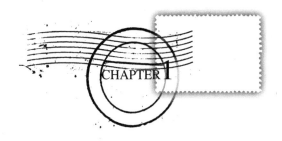

FROM A LAND OF
NO RETURN

Isolation is the sum total of wretchedness to a man.
THOMAS CARLYLE (1795–1881)

A message is written, addressed to a speck on the other side of the globe, stamped and slid casually into a hole in the wall: a commonplace act of faith. Just why can we be so certain that letters like these will reach their destination? Because it's been happening like that for 200 years, delivered by sailing ships, bush horsemen, rattling coaches, precarious flying machines, and in World War II, even a Japanese bomber. It's quite a story.

With the dawn of instant communication, the gentle letter may have lost its unique power to stave off isolation and despair. But for two centuries, the handwritten missive was paramount, a salve to isolation for each wretched convict and homesick digger. The evolution of a sprawling postal network connected these strands of humanity across an arid continent spanning 4000 kilometres from east to west, and six times that distance to the place once called Home. Through bushfire and drought, devastating world wars and crippling depressions, the lines of communication were never severed. The mail got through.

The instinct for contact must have ached large in the hearts of every convict, soldier and merchant who left Portsmouth on 13 May 1787. The voyage, conveying one of the largest armadas in history, had lasted more than eight months, and its cargo of more than 1400 men, women and children had endured freak storms, lice infestation, dysentery and scurvy while crammed in foul conditions aboard the 11 ships. Landing on 17 January 1788, the predestined settlement to Botany Bay was quickly rejected by Captain Arthur Phillip, the colony's governor-designate. As a port for safe anchorage it was less than ideal, the soil appeared to be of poor quality and the supply of fresh water was inadequate. A search party was dispatched and eight days later the British flag was raised in Port Jackson.

For those who were literate, writing provided a refuge from the inhospitable environment and harshness of daily life. Their letters would form the first history of the colony, documenting a radical social experiment which was to continue for almost a century. For most, however, a two-and-a-half-year silence lay ahead before any familiar word from the outside world penetrated their isolation.

National Library of Australia researcher Judy Cannon marvels at the personal glimpses into early convict life gleaned from even the briefest of scrawls. 'Something of the writer's character—although a writer knew an official was likely to read it—seeps through, along with a sense of how an individual really felt about being transported to the other side of the world, aware that return was unlikely,' she says. 'An acute need for news of home and families and perhaps reassurance that their own still care about them troubles the reader; there is a haunting echo of loneliness.'

Less than two months after the First Fleet dropped anchor in Port Jackson, Phillip received what is widely accepted as the colony's first letter, from HMS *Supply*. The message was a progress report from Second Lieutenant Philip Gidley King, who, no sooner having arrived in New South Wales with the First Fleet, had been dispatched with 15 convicts and seven guards to set up a second penal colony at Norfolk Island. In doing so, King George III could be reassured the island, possessing what was thought to be one of the finest supplies of timber in the world, remained beyond the clutches of the French. One of the first civilian letters, penned by an unknown female convict, records the impact of the departure of the *Supply* to Norfolk Island:

> The separation of several of us to an uninhabited island was like a second transportation. In short, every one is so taken up with their own misfortunes that they have no pity to bestow upon others. All our letters are examined by an officer, but a friend takes this for me privately. The ships sail tomorrow.

When the First Fleet vessel the *Alexander* set sail for the return voyage to England on 13 July, among the cargo was the first mail ever processed on Australian shores: Governor Phillip's first dispatch to the British Government, a handful of private correspondence, and a bundle of letters addressed to the French Ambassador in London, regarding a French navy officer with an impressive-sounding name. Although the Governor of New South Wales and Jean-François de Galaup, Comte de La Pérouse, never met, Phillip agreed to the explorer's request to deliver his correspondence as a gesture of British goodwill. Having remained in Botany Bay with HMS *Sirius* and the fleet's transport ships on Phillip's orders, Captain John Hunter witnessed the arrival of La Pérouse's scientific expedition at Botany Bay just six days after the First Fleet's arrival, although the treacherous conditions prevented the Frenchman from anchoring for a further two days. La Pérouse accepted his runner-up status with equanimity and Hunter duly conveyed the letters back to Port Jackson. They were to be the last official records of the French expedition. On 10 March, La Pérouse bid Hunter farewell, set sail and disappeared. The fate of *La Boussole* and *L'Astrolabe* was to remain a mystery for another 38 years, until evidence of shipwreck was discovered off Vanikolo Island in the New Hebrides in 1826.

Back in Sydney, the colony's initial progress was less than auspicious. According to the records of the first Judge-Advocate, Captain David Collins, the Governor was obliged to read the riot act to his bedraggled convict mob less than a fortnight after landing in Port Jackson:

The convicts were order'd to sit down, and the Governor made an harangue to them, telling them he had try'd them hitherto to see how they were disposed, that he was thoroughly convinced they were many of them incorrigible, and that he was convinced nothing but severity w'd have any effect upon them to induce them to behave properly.

4

He also assure'd them if they attempted by night to get into the women's tents there were positive orders for the centry to fire upon them; that they had been very idle, wandering ab't the country, and not more than 200 out of 600 convicts were at work; that the industrious sh'd not labour for the idle; if they did not work they sh'd not eat; that in England if thieving poultry was to be punish'd w'h death in consequence of their being so easily supply'd, but here a fowl was of the utmost consequence to the settlement, as well as every other species of stock, as they were reserved for breed, therefore stealing the most trifling article of stock or provissions sh'd be punish'd with death; that however such severity might militate against his humanity and feelings, yet justice demanded such rigid execution of the laws, and they might implicitly rely upon justice taking place. Their labour w'd not be equal to that a husbandman in England endures who has a wife and family to provide for; they w'd never be work'd beyond their abilities, but everyone sh'd contribute his share in order to render himself and the community at large happy and comfortable; as soon as the nature of the settlement w'd admit of, that they sh'd be employ'd erecting houses for the different officers, the soldiers, and afterwards for themselves. After this harangue they were dismiss'd in the same form in which they were assembl'd. The Governor had a cold collation under a large tent, to which the general officers were invited.

The cattle, sheep and sacks of seed brought with the fleet proved a pitiful foundation for the genesis of a civilisation. Tended by novice convict farmers weakened by sickness and

5

starvation, the first crops failed. By the end of the first year of settlement, food rations had been cut back to subsistence level. And despite the ever-present deterrent of flogging and hanging, theft and assault were rife in a brute society where each and every wretched being was struggling for survival. When the British Government received a letter from Phillip saying the provision of more women was 'absolutely necessary' as a civilising influence on the colony, Sir Evan Nepean, the Permanent Under-Secretary of State for the Home Department, agreed. Parliament needed little convincing that the presence of ladies—no matter how far that term might be stretched—would not only prevent the male convict population from engaging in 'gross irregularities', it would also supply the colony with much-needed human breeding stock. More than 200 female prostitutes, petty thieves, grifters and vagabonds, with at least five suckling infants in tow, were duly cleared from London's overflowing putrid prisons. The desperate flotsam were herded onto the *Lady Juliana*, and, along with fresh supplies and a further 800-odd convicts, a second fleet of six ships left England on 29 July 1789.

With a ratio of one female to every five males in the colony, a shipload of rugged young women sailing into Sydney Harbour on what history would dub the Floating Brothel would surely fill the heart of many a man watching from the shore with an instant lusty zeal. And indeed, more than half the women on board were chronologically ideal breeding stock, aged between 20 and 29. All but 23 were under the age of 39. But if the ladies of the *Lady Juliana* were expecting a welcoming ball, they were to be sorely disappointed. On the cusp of total collapse, the colony was expecting salvation in the form of supplies, not more mouths to feed. Moreover, after 10 months at sea, many of the women, including seven bearing newborn infants, looked more starved and disease-ridden than the hungry convicts on shore. Phillip soon learnt that the Second Fleet's principal supply ship, the *Guardian*, stocked with most of the expedition's provisions, had struck ice. She would not be making it to Sydney Cove.

The one saving grace on the *Lady Juliana* was letters. Watkin Tench, a 31-year-old Marine officer and son of a Cheshire dancing instructor, was on the first boat which rowed out to reach the vessel. In his account of the settlement of Port Jackson, which was later to become a best-seller for the London publisher Debrett, Tench described how hardened criminals wept, as two and a half years of interminable silence from the home country were shattered.

> 'Letters, letters!' was the cry. They were produced, and torn open in trembling agitation. News burst upon us like meridian splendor on a blind man. We were overwhelmed with it: public, private, general, and particular. Nor was it until some days had elapsed, that we were able to methodise it, or reduce it into form.

Among those such as Tench with sufficient education to comprehend the significance of social and political events in Europe, much of the news from home would have astounded them. When the passengers of the First Fleet set sail from Portsmouth in May 1787, to all public knowledge their king was sane. Within four months of the fleet's departure, rumours had spread widely that George III was gabbling constantly and incoherently, and had taken to the habit of shaking hands with trees, in the mistaken belief he was meeting the King of Prussia. As England went about transporting another 38,000 slaves to the New World each year, William Wilberforce and the Prime Minister, William Pitt the Younger, had taken a stand in Parliament, introducing a motion for the abolition of the slave trade. Fletcher Christian had led a mutiny on HMS *Bounty*, setting its captain, William Bligh, and 18 sailors adrift in the South Pacific. A newspaper called *The Times* had hit the streets of London, and by the time the Second Fleet sailed into Port Jackson, the paper's editor, John Walter, was already facing a year's imprisonment in Newgate Gaol, having been convicted of libel against the Duke of York. The introduction of designated left and right shoes had taken London's footwear fashion by storm, with the novel concept of shoelaces following close behind. The ladies would have been horrified to learn that their countrywomen's buttocks were no longer safe in public, as a knife-wielding stalker dubbed The Monster terrorised London, reportedly choosing only the most beautiful young female rumps to jab. With the promise of a £100 reward for his capture, armed vigilantes had taken to the streets. And the gentlemen would have been relieved to hear that the rules for cricket had finally been set, with the opening of Lord's and the foundation of the Marylebone Cricket Club.

Letters were also bursting with news of political upheaval among England's neighbours and former colonies. The storming of the Bastille in Paris heralded the beginning of the French Revolution, an event signalling the death of unlimited monarchies; worse still, it had scarpered much-anticipated plans for the English cricket team's first overseas tour. The

Ottoman Empire had declared war on Russia. The ink was dry on the Constitution of the United States and the people of America had voted in George Washington as their first president. Reports of newfangled ideas emerging from this New World would have intrigued the First Fleet settlers; an observance called Thanksgiving appeared to have supplanted the overarching social significance of Christmas, while a distilled beverage called bourbon—made from corn of all things—was threatening to topple rum as the tipple of choice. And a founding father of that New World had made his timeless observation: that in this life, nothing can be said to be certain except death and taxes. Benjamin Franklin, who uttered this depressingly frank observation a year before his own demise, was speaking from experience. Some 25 years earlier, he had unsuccessfully attempted to thwart the British Empire's attempt to lob its first revenue-raising tax on the colonies—the stamp tax. Franklin went on to be the driving force behind the creation of the United States Postal Service in 1775, but the stamp tax stayed.

While taxes were yet to become an irrefutable fact of life in New South Wales, death was omnipresent, no more so than when the full horror of the Second Fleet's voyage slowly unravelled over the course of June 1790. The exhilaration of the mailbags was soon extinguished, as the remaining ships arrived and disgorged their grim cargo. The First Fleet had lost just 48 passengers during its eight-month voyage, a death rate of about 3 per cent. More than 270 perished on the second voyage—almost a third of the convicts the fleet was carrying. It was to be the highest mortality rate in Australian transportation history. Some

161 men, women and boys died on the *Neptune* alone, while virtually all the survivors were either on the point of death or too weak to work. An article published in the *Sydney Cove Chronicle* on 30 June 1790, titled 'Diabolical Condition of the Convicts Thereon', reported:

> The landing of those who remained alive despite their misuse upon the recent voyage, could not fail to horrify those who watched. As they came on shore, these wretched people were hardly able to move hand or foot. Such as could not carry themselves upon their legs, crawled upon all fours. Those, who, through their afflictions, were not able to move, were thrown over the side of the ships; as sacks of flour would be thrown, into the small boats.

What had gone so appallingly awry? The *Lady Juliana* and her five fellow Second Fleet vessels had been contracted out by the British Government to private operators. Camden, Calvert & King was a company which had made its fortune and staked its reputation on the transportation of slaves to America. The company had been paid a flat rate for every convict it took on board, regardless of whether they arrived dead or alive at the other end. Government regulations stipulated that prisoners should be supplied with adequate food and given access to fresh air each day, yet many in the Second Fleet had spent the voyage shackled in chains below decks where dysentery, typhoid, scurvy and smallpox took hold. Virtually all the surviving convicts disembarking on Australian shores were severely malnourished.

Once news of the convict death fleet reached England,

popular outcry among emancipists demanded an inquest. Charges were laid against some of the crew but not a single conviction ensued. Quite possibly it was Governor Phillip himself who dobbed in the slave ship company to the British authorities. A letter from an unnamed female convict written in Sydney Cove on 24 July 1790, suggests as much:

> Oh! If you had but seen the shocking sight of the poor creatures that came out in the three ships it would make your heart bleed . . . They were almost dead, very few could stand, and they were obliged to fling them as you would goods, and hoist them out of the ships, they were so feeble; and they died ten or twelve a day when they first landed . . . The Governor was very angry, and scolded the captains a great deal, and, I heard, intended to write to London about it, for I heard him say it was murdering them. It, to be sure, was a melancholy sight.

The letter was more than a year old by the time it reached the pages of *London's Morning Chronicle*.

The letters of these early colonists, both free and bonded, serve as the first history of Australian white settlement— letters which paint a harsh picture of Australian life, yet not lacking in optimism. The level of literacy among convicts has been historically underestimated, and all prisoners were granted free delivery of their letters. Authorities were clearly aware of the rehabilitation possibilities associated with personal correspondence, with taskmasters such as Fremantle Prison's superintendent, Thomas H. Dixon, decreeing that prisoners might write one letter upon arrival and subsequently another every two months. They were also permitted to receive one prepaid letter every two months, but were warned that 'all letters of an improper, or evil tendency either to, or from the prisoner, or containing "Slang" or other objectionable expressions will be suppressed'.

According to Australian academics Stephen Nicholas and Peter Shergold, the proportion of skilled, semi-skilled and unskilled workers among the early convicts differed little from the general British workforce from which it was drawn. Yet the overall literacy level of Australian convicts was significantly higher than the general literacy of the British and Irish working class. A 'labour aristocracy' among convicts—those with high levels of literacy and skills—was thought to comprise almost one in five convicts by the 1840s, affording this group greater work autonomy and opportunity for generating private income outside their hours of indentured servitude. Certainly, as the industrial revolution gathered momentum in England throughout the early 19th century, many convicts were working fewer hours than their free counterparts back home, and in a far healthier natural environment. By the mid-19th century, Australia had a higher fertility rate and significantly lower child mortality rate than most of the industrial cities of Britain. And after the subsistence rations which characterised the early years of the colony were raised, convicts were generally well fed, if only to maintain their productivity. The weekly government rations for male convicts in New South Wales in 1811 was 7 pounds (3 kilos) of salt beef, 4 pounds (1.8 kilos) of pork, 6 pounds (2.7 kilos) of wheat, and 15 pounds (6.8 kilos) of corn.

The threat of harsh punishment for transgression, however, played heavily on their minds, particularly those assigned to unskilled, labour-intensive work. The crack of the cat o' nine tails and the hangman's noose were ever-present incentives to maintain productivity, and in the early days, justice, administered through a court-martial system, was swift and erratic. Samuel Payton, a 20-year-old convict, wrote this letter to his mother in England on the eve of his execution, in June 1790:

> My dear mother! With what agony of soul do I dedicate the last few moments of my life, to bid you an eternal adieu! My doom being irrevocably fixed, and ere this hour tomorrow I shall have quitted this vale of wretchedness. I have at last fallen an unhappy, though just, victim of my follies. Banish from your memory all my former indiscretions and let the cheering hope of a happy meeting hereafter console you.

According to the records of Sydney's first Surgeon-General, John White, Payton was sentenced to hang for 'feloniously entering the marquee of Lieutenant Fuzer, on the night of the fourth of June, and stealing from thence some shirts, stockings and combs'. Caught red-handed by another officer, Payton was beaten senseless. On 24 June, he and another convict, Edward Corbett, were 'brought to the fatal tree'. Corbett had been found guilty of stealing a frock, and suspected, but not convicted, of making off with four cows—which at this early point comprised the colony's entire herd. In his journal, White conceded the cattle had in all probability simply strayed off, 'in this endless wild, as to be irrecoverably lost'. White writes poignantly of the contrition both men displayed at their makeshift gallows:

They (particularly Payton) addressed the convicts in a pathetic, eloquent, and well-directed speech. He acknowledged the justice of his sentence, a sentence, which (he said) he had long deserved. He added that he hoped and trusted that the ignominious death he was about to suffer would serve as a caution and warning to those who saw and heard him. They both prayed most fervently, begging forgiveness of an offended GOD. They likewise hoped that those whom they had injured would not only forgive them, as they themselves did all mankind, but offer up their prayers to a merciful REDEEMER that, though so great sinners, they might be received into that bliss which the good and virtuous only can either deserve or expect.

They were now turned off, and in the agonising moments of the separation of the soul from the body seemed to embrace each other.

Letters from the grave travelled the high seas in both directions. The length of the eight-month journey upon which they were carried was only to improve with the introduction of clipper ships in the 1840s. When mail arrived for every officer but George Harris in August 1804, the man who would later go on to co-found Hobart Town sat down and penned a plaintive letter to his brother, begging for a word from home. His mother obliged, but the sending and reciprocation of the correspondence had taken almost three years.

The letters which formed the earliest narrative history of a fledgling society were not solely focused on the hardship and despair of convict life. For many, transportation promised a fresh start, and once their sentence had been served, a chance to better their position in a society free from tradition and class strictures. Fremantle convict Griffith Bowyer wrote to his parents telling them he liked 'this Colony very well' and had been assured by the Governor that good conduct and willing industriousness would be rewarded with an early ticket of leave. And upon earning his freedom, Bowyer wrote, a man 'may do very well if he is only steady and keeps out of bad company'.

For many of the female convicts, life in the colony was an improvement on their impoverished existences in the old country and the fetid conditions of London's prisons. An analysis of female convict data by Australian historian Deborah Oxley has found that far from being a class of professional criminals, the majority of females flagged for transportation had no prior convictions and had most likely been driven to transgress through low wages or the inability to find paid work. The overwhelming majority had been found guilty of crimes of property theft, and well over half of these types of offences involved stealing basic necessities such as clothing, yarn, pots and pans, bedding and food.

For those prepared to loosen the strictures of Georgian morals, better food and sleeping arrangements could be secured on the voyage out, by agreeing to become a 'wife' of one of the ship's crew. The sex trade was flourishing as much in Georgian England as it was on the floating brothels of the early fleets, or on the mud of Sydney's rudimentary streets.

Mary Haydock was just 14 years old when, as an orphan runaway disguised as a boy, she was caught stealing a horse and sentenced to transportation for seven years. She arrived in New South Wales on the *Royal Admiral* in October 1792, and was immediately assigned to nursemaid duties in the household of Major Francis Grose.

> My Dear aunt
>
> We arrived here on the 7th and I hope it will answer better than we expected for I write this on Board of ship but it looks a pleasant place—Enough we shall but have 4 pair of trowser to make a week and we shall have one pound of rice a week and 4 pound of pork besides Greens and other Vegetaibles the tell me I am for life wich The Governor told me I was but for 7 years wich Grives me very much to think of it but I will watch every oppertunity to get away in too or 3 years But I will make my self as happy as I Can In my Pressent and unhappy situation . . . Mr Scot Took 2 Ginnues of me and said he would get me My Libberty . . .

Possibly it was the '2 Ginnues' which secured Mary's freedom less than two years after writing this letter. She went on to marry and bear seven children to Thomas Reibey, a wealthy merchant trader, and upon his death in 1811, assumed sole control of his numerous business enterprises. Mary Reibey became a woman of considerable wealth, opening warehouses in George Street, extending her husband's shipping operations, and amassing an impressive real estate portfolio in and around Sydney. She gained added respect in Sydney society for her charitable works, devotion to the church and promoting education. In 1825 she was appointed a founding governor of the Free Grammar School, which was later to become Sydney Grammar. Upon her retirement, she built a house in

Newtown, where she lived until her death at age 78. She had outlived five of her seven children. One of her grandsons, also named Thomas Reibey, would go on to become the 11th premier of Tasmania.

Today, Mary Reibey's face features on the Australian $20 note, an attestation of the radical transformation that was indeed possible in this precarious new world.

As Thomas Carlyle so aptly observed: 'Man is, properly speaking, based upon hope; he has no other possession but hope; this world of his is emphatically the place of hope.'

CHAPTER 2

A MOST USEFUL MAN

Sydney's wharves were in chaos. In little more than 20 years since the First Fleet's arrival, New South Wales had grown from a single straggling penal settlement to a bustling colony of more than 10,000 people. But while the arrival of ships had become a regular occurrence at Sydney Cove, the commotion with which they were greeted remained the same. Crews were mobbed as eager settlers and freed convicts swooped on the ships' decks, desperate to retrieve letters and news from home. Such sophisticated a concept as a postal service, which Charles I had instigated in England more than a century and a half earlier with the opening to the public of the Royal Mails, had not been foreseen in a place that had started as an isolated dumping ground for incorrigible law-breakers.

In the colony's early years, the handwritten official messages which criss-crossed the town daily were delivered in an ad hoc fashion, by constable or convict. Public news was disseminated through the town crier or posted notice, and what little private mail existed was unofficially carried by the constabulary, with the encouragement of a small unofficial fee. By 1803, however, a private delivery service linking Sydney to Rose Hill was established, with letters carried along the Parramatta River at an advertised rate of twopence each. A supply route between the two settlements had been forged some 14 years earlier, with the completion in October 1789 of the colony's first ferry. Built on the site where Sydney's Customs House stands today, the 10-ton *Rose Hill Packet* was crude and cumbersome, and could take anywhere up to a week to complete the 48-kilometre round trip.

If maintaining communication within the colony required patience, reaching the outside world took forbearance and faith. Before setting sail for England, captains were required by law to advertise their date and time of departure in the *Sydney Gazette*. Citizens would then have to lodge their letters at a designated place—often a private residence—and pay a fee determined by the captain, who gave no guarantees of a safe delivery into the English or Irish postal systems at the other end. If Government House had possessed a complaints counter, by 1809 it would have been overrun with livid customers reporting missing letters and filched parcels. The infamous Rum Rebellion a year earlier had dispatched the colony's fourth governor, William Bligh, to Hobart on HMS *Porpoise*. Sydney was consequently under the temporary guardianship of Lieutenant-Governor Joseph Foveaux, and it was he who made the decision to engage a former convict to restore order on the wharves. Thus an announcement ran in the *Sydney Gazette* on 30 April 1809:

> Complaints having been made to the Lieutenant Governor, that numerous Frauds have been committed by Individuals repairing on board Ships, on their arrival at this Port, and personating others, by which they have obtained possession of Letters and Parcels to the great injury of those for whom they were intended, the Lieutenant Governor, in order to prevent the practice of such Frauds in future, has been pleased to establish an Office, at which all Parcels and Letters addressed to the Inhabitants of this Colony shall be deposited, previous to their distribution: Which Office shall be under the direction of Mr Isaac Nichols (Assistant to the Naval officer), who has entered into Security for the faithful discharge of the trust reposed in him.

The appointment of Isaac Nichols as Australia's first postmaster was a shrewd choice on the part of Foveaux. The son of a Wiltshire textile worker, Nichols had survived the grim journey of the Second Fleet, and quickly impressed the colony's second Governor, John Hunter, with his intelligence, trustworthiness and that rarest of qualities in 19th-century Sydney, sobriety. His purported crime had been the theft of a donkey, a since discredited although still widely held belief. According to direct descendant Graeme Nichols, the original charge sheet showed that the founder of the Australian postal service was convicted 'on suspicion of stealing a brass pot and violent suspicion of stealing a silver watch'. After serving his seven-year sentence, during which time he became chief overseer of Sydney's convict labour gangs, Nichols was granted 50 acres (20 hectares), a parcel of land in the Concord area which would develop into a 1400-acre (570-hectare) property portfolio within his lifetime. By 1809, this emancipist esquire, who had sided with the insurrectionists during the previous year's rebellion, was the owner of a thriving shipbuilding business, the respectable proprietor of the Jolly Roger inn on George Street, and the resident of a substantial home further down the road, on the corner of George Street and Circular Quay. A month before he assumed his decade-long role as defender of the mails, Nichols was appointed superintendent of public works and assistant to the Naval Officer. It did not take long for Governor Lachlan Macquarie, who arrived in the colony eight months after the postmaster's appointment, to publicly proclaim Nichols 'a most zealous, active and useful man'.

Nichols's services to the colony did not come cheaply, however. Initially, his duties consisted simply of collecting the mail from incoming ships' captains, then passing the articles on to recipients for a fee of a shilling per letter and up to 5 shillings per parcel—the equivalent of about $30 in today's money. It was a monopoly—and a government-endorsed private enterprise—in its purest form, with the postmaster operating the business from a ground-floor room in his comparatively lavish George Street home. Upon a ship's entry, Nichols advertised in the Sydney Gazette, listing the recipients of all incoming mail. Soldiers, however, got special discounts, taking possession of their letters for just a penny each, while the local dignitaries of the town received personal deliveries from Nichols himself at no extra charge. The postmaster was, after all, keen to build his business network and maintain his myriad entrepreneurial interests in agriculture, shipbuilding and spirituous liquids. It was a symbiotic relationship which would endure until his death in 1819, when the post office was transferred from Nichols's gracious home to a small building on the Kings Wharf. Perhaps seeking to emulate his predecessor, George Panton soon relocated what had come to be known as 'the Post Office' to his private home at Bunkers Hill in The Rocks. But a cannonade of complaints quickly forced Panton to move the post office back to Kings Wharf.

Mail delivery was to remain in private hands for 16 years, until the New South Wales Legislative Council passed the first postal act in 1825, allowing the government to assume direct control of the colony's postal services. The Governor was given the power to appoint postmasters throughout the colony and determine how much they were to be paid. By the late 1820s, Sydney's post office, now based in Bent Street, had become a focal point of the town and a major interchange for coaches, horses and contractors. Australia's first letter carriers appeared in 1828 and the familiar ring of the postie's hand bell joined the general clamour of Sydney's streets.

By 1830 the post office had outgrown its modest accommodation and the decision was made to relocate the bustling headquarters of the colony's fledgling postal service to a two-storey building on George Street, on the site where the grand Italian Renaissance-inspired General Post Office stands today. Panton had died a year earlier, and a County Limerick landowner, James Raymond, who had arrived in Sydney with his wife and nine children in 1826 after fleeing hungry mutinous Irish locals, assumed control. The following year the first letter boxes appeared in Sydney's streets and soon a twice-daily clearance and local delivery system was in place. A flat postal rate of twopence was introduced for delivery within the town's boundaries—a rate which would remain unchanged for the next 80 years. Despite such progress, the postal service remained somewhat inefficient. Until prepaid postage became compulsory in the 1850s, most people preferred to make the addressee pay. The mail would be cleared from the town's letter boxes and delivered to the post office, where each item would be weighed and, once the distance it needed to travel was factored in, a price calculated. The letter carrier was then obliged to call at the addressee's residence when someone was at home, for the cash-on-delivery system to work. The practice of expecting the addressee to pay may not necessarily have been an indication of the townsfolk's general tight-fistedness, however. According to a theory put forward by the Australian Heritage Council, the resistance to prepaid mail may have been rooted in one of the earliest examples of snobbery: a prepaid letter implied that the addressee could not afford to pay the postage, and the recipient-paid postage system certainly was expensive. It was not unheard of for people to glance at the handwriting, identify the author and send the letter carrier on his way, satisfied in the knowledge that the friend or family member was at least still alive. Senders did show consideration, though. As letters were charged according to weight, the use of more than one sheet of paper was to be avoided and the practice of cross writing—where the sender would fill a page with text, then turn the paper on its side and continue writing horizontally—was common, even though it made the letter somewhat more difficult for the recipient to read.

The most concerted attempt to persuade the colony's population to embrace a sender-pays postal service came in 1838, with the *New South Wales Government Gazette* reporting on 14 November that the post office had begun offering prepaid embossed letter sheets for sale, for 'one payment of one shilling and three pence per dozen, including all charges for paper and delivery'. The idea was the brainchild of James Raymond, whose title had been upgraded to Postmaster-General several years before. Raymond had been inspired by the English social reformer Rowland Hill, the founder of what was to become the model for public education among England's emerging middle classes. As secretary of Britain's South Australian Colonisation Commission, Hill was at the time working to establish Australia's first colony of free settlers, which had recently become known as the town of Adelaide. But it was his famous private pamphlet 'Post Office Reform: its Importance and Practicability', circulated throughout England in 1837, which captured the imagination of Sydney's postmaster. Hill's pamphlet, which argued that his own country's expensive and inefficient postal service was the result of a labour-intensive pay-on-delivery system, called for 'low and uniform rates' calculated solely on weight, and regardless of distance. He called for universal one-penny postage, with prepayment through the adoption of stamped covers or postage stamps. Despite various parliamentarians dismissing Hill's ideas as 'wild' and 'preposterous', by 1839, he had secured a two-year contract to reform Britain's postal system.

Australia, however, got there first, by a matter of a few months. Raymond's prepaid stamp sheets, which doubled as envelopes and could be used for delivery anywhere within the town limits, presented an enormous potential saving to the colony's letter writers, slashing the cost of sending local mail by almost half. The product was cheap, efficient and a world first. Yet through public resistance towards a sender-pays system, the prepaid stamp sheets were a spectacular failure. In May 1840, Hill's first adhesive postage stamps were distributed in Britain, featuring an elegant engraving of a young Queen Victoria. Another decade would pass before New South Wales attained the equivalent of that famed Penny Black.

Outside Sydney's boundaries, the mail was still carried privately or by constables. During his term as postmaster, George Panton had begun encouraging settlers to tender for mail delivery contracts. By March 1828, a daily horse-powered post service was operating from Sydney to Parramatta and Liverpool, a twice-weekly service was being provided to Windsor and Campbelltown, and a weekly service to Penrith and Bathurst. Letters to Newcastle, which had been established as a penal colony of secondary punishment for exceptionally incorrigible convicts in 1804, made their way by ship. While rail would undoubtedly prove the most efficient way to transport mail by the end of the century, inland settlements separated by vast tracts of bush were still being serviced by horse and mail coach well into the 1920s. Across hostile terrain, flooded river and parched desert, the one contrivance which held the power to stave off isolation got through, at least most of the time. And the individuals charged with the task frequently made the headlines of the early newspapers, their tales of intrepid exploits and true grit fashioning local heroes from the mailmen and coach drivers.

The ceaseless search for arable land had motivated competing Tasmanian settlers John Batman and John Pascoe Fawkner to seperately cross Bass Strait in 1835, thereby co-founding Melbourne on the lower reaches of the Yarra River. Although the Port Phillip district was to remain under the governance of New South Wales until 1851, Victoria's early settlers had been happy to entrust their postal affairs to Batman for the first two years until Edward J. Foster was officially appointed postmaster in 1837. The following year an entrepreneur by the name of John Hawdon forged the first overland mail route between Sydney and Melbourne. Hawdon had already made a name for himself, having driven the first herd of cattle from New South Wales to Melbourne, and another from Goulburn to the newly established settlement of Adelaide, where the founding residents were on the brink of starvation. The contract for the 640-kilometre overland journey by packhorse between Melbourne and Yass, with the mail then being carried on to Sydney by coach, took between 12 and 14 days, then the longest mail run in the British Empire.

This crucial Melbourne to Sydney mail run turned pioneering mailman John Conway Bourke into a postal legend. On New Year's Day in 1838, the 23-year-old stockman had set out from Melbourne for Yass, through the usual rugged and unforgiving wilderness. But as he hit the Murray River, he was attacked by hostile Aborigines, his horse was speared and he found himself stranded on the river bank. Bourke stripped, grabbed the mailbags and began to swim for his life, no doubt hoping he would be able to find a fresh mount and new clothes on the other side. But on the eastern bank a pack of wild dogs gave chase, in what was probably the first documented case of canine persecution of a postie on Australian soil. Bourke clambered up a tree where he remained for a considerable chilly time, before a settler spotted him. Assuming Bourke was an escaped convict, the settler aimed his rifle at the tree.

'Don't fire!' the hapless mailman hollered. 'My name's Bourke. I am Her Majesty's Mails!'

To which the bemused settler reportedly replied: 'Don't think much of your uniform.'

John Conway Bourke saved the mail that day but not his modesty. His reputation was forged upon the thousands of gruelling kilometres he rode in his lifetime, pioneering the mail trails before ending his days delivering telegrams in Melbourne on foot.

The Ararat to Ballarat route in Victoria made a celebrity of mailman William Jones, who saved the mail with a daring swim with six horses across the flooded Hopkins River. Getting the mail through to Victoria's inland settlements by land remained a daunting challenge for some time, with the locations of Victoria's founding post offices—at Port Fairy, Geelong, Warrnambool and Portland—demonstrating the colony's reliance on boat deliveries for some decades.

By the mid-1840s, mail contractors were not only dealing with inhospitable terrain and stroppy locals. The increasingly common sight of letters littering a track, a stranded cart and a trembling mailman bound with rope heralded the era of the bushranger. For two years, John Ross delivered the Portland to Melbourne mail before he decided to take a stand. In 1851 he had been held up along the 400-kilometre trail three times already, and the fourth turned out to be the last straw. At the sight of the bushranger, he decided to make a run for it, a decision that nearly cost him his life. Ross made it to Melbourne still clutching the mail bags, but a hole in his hat showed the bushranger's bullet had missed his skull by a couple of centimetres. His nerves were shot, and on medical advice, he made that fateful Portland to Melbourne dash the swan song of his career in mail delivery. Quite possibly this earned him the distinction of becoming the first victim of work-related stress within the Australian postal services.

Raiding the mailbags proved something of a lucky dip for Australia's first bushrangers, however. During the trial over a hold-up of the Royal Mails on the Melbourne to Port Fairy run in 1851, the judge remained unimpressed by William Green's plea for clemency, based on the grounds the stolen mailbags had yielded more love letters than valuables. He was sentenced to 15 years' imprisonment. Later that year, news of the discovery of gold in the hills near Ballarat and Bathurst would overnight make the job of bushranging a considerably more lucrative career.

The sheer expanse of Queensland, along with its treacherous razorback ridges, gave the colony the reputation of possessing some of the most challenging early mail routes. The first track over the Great Dividing Range, via Spicer's Gap, which had been discovered by stockman Henry Alphen in 1847, required one determined pioneer and 36 bullocks to haul the earliest drays loaded with supplies and mail to the fertile agricultural lands of the Darling Downs on the other side. In 1824, the colony had been little more than a single ramshackle penal settlement on the Brisbane River known as Moreton Bay. But as exploration and transport opened up the interior, myriad settlements followed and so did the mail. The northern colony remained under the direct administration of New South Wales for the first 35 years of its existence, only becoming the independent Queensland in 1859. William Whyte had become the colony's first Commandant's Clerk and Postmaster in April 1830, and until Moreton Bay's function as a penal settlement was terminated 12 years later, the postmaster role remained a military one. It would not be until 1852 that the colony would receive its first full-time civilian postmaster, Captain James Barney. By the mid-1840s, however, a regular steamship service began operation, ferrying passengers, mail and freight between Sydney and Brisbane. In 1845, the colony's second post office opened. Mushrooming settlements in the Brisbane area that were subsequently creeping southwards made The Springs post office, located south-west of Too-woomba, a pivotal outpost. The town would later be renamed Drayton, in honour of the many horse-driven drays which passed through the settlement in those early days.

Western Australia's isolation, immeasurable distance from the eastern colonies and sparse population delayed the founding of a regular postal service for some time. Fortified with a weekly salary of one guinea, however, by 1830 the colony's first letter carrier was making the 19-kilometre trek between Fremantle and Perth three times a week, with postmasters James Purkis and Lionel Samson overseeing the operations at either end. According to Marcella Hunter's comprehensive history of Australian postal services, the post office Purkis had taken charge of was nothing more than a humble box in a corner of a Perth storehouse. It nevertheless grew into the town's first General Post Office within three years, with branches at Fremantle and Albany, where Sarah Lyttleton became Western Australia's first postmistress. For much of the 19th century, all mail destined for Western Australians was delivered by ship to Albany. Contractors would converge on the wharf each month, collect the mailbags, then make the 400-kilometre journey north to Perth, where citizens were charged threepence per letter upon collection. Until its declaration as a town in 1832 by Governor James Stirling, Albany was known as King George Sound, and the reassuring clatter of the horse-drawn carts rattling into Perth became known as the Sound Mail. The vast size of Western Australia discouraged all but the most enterprising of mail contractors, but by the mid-19th century, a 204-kilometre mail route was nevertheless linking Bunbury and Vasse, while an 85-kilometre run was keeping the communication lines open between Perth and York.

To Western Australia's immediate south-east, thick bush and desert were daunting factors in the haulage of inland mail from the model colony of free settlers in Adelaide. The never-ending cycle of drought and flood ravaged the rough bush tracks the mail coaches relied upon, and many a time mail contractors were forced to abandon their transport and carry on by foot. Like Australia's first postmaster, Isaac Nichols, Adelaide storekeeper Thomas Gilbert operated the town's first post office from his home, situated on the banks of the Torrens River. The new business sideline earned him an annual stipend of £30. He handed over to the colony's first

Postmaster-General, Lieutenant Henry Watts, less than two years later. Watts also took the option of 'working from home', at an ideal location on the corner of King William Street and North Terrace. As the population spread, post offices in Port Adelaide, Port Lincoln, Willunga and Encounter Bay soon followed.

From the outset South Australians enjoyed bargain postal rates. Despite the enormous effort of getting mail into the interior, inland postage charges were set at a uniform threepence irrespective of weight, under the *Post Office Act 1839*. Although no formal contracts existed, Adelaide to Sydney services by ship were even cheaper, with letters costing just a penny each, a sum which was passed directly on to the ships' captains as gratuity. The thrift of Adelaide's earliest postal system did not always guarantee reliability, however. The paltry penny-a-letter levy meant some captains, once out on the open seas, were more motivated to cast the mailbags overboard, to save bothering themselves with organising collection once docked in Sydney. According to Marcella Hunter's history, it was not even unheard of for captains to simply 'forget' the outbound mail altogether, leaving the postmaster to hastily procure a row boat, collect the abandoned bags off the beach and brave the open waters to deliver the mail to the departing vessels.

Shipping also played a vital role in the development of postal services on Van Diemen's Land. In its earliest days, the colony relied on whaling and sealing ships crossing Bass Strait for mail deliveries, an arrangement which relied exclusively on private enterprise. It was not uncommon for captains to accept in-kind payments. Records show that on at least one occasion, the government mail was only handed over to Van Diemen's Land officials after they presented 30 caskets of salted meat to the ship's captain. The progress of Van Diemen's Land's own postal service kept pace with Sydney's. The colony appointed its first postmaster, John Beaumont, in 1812, just three years after Isaac Nichols was first charged with restoring order on Sydney's wharves, and some 18 years before a colony of secondary punishment was established on the island at Port Arthur. In 1816, the Hobart Town Gazette ran reports of a seemingly impossible route forged all the way from Launceston in the north, with Tom Stocker and his partner Richardson tackling flooded terrain which was 'almost a complete body of water' to reach Hobart with supplies and mail. Lobbying from the colony's third postmaster, John Collicott, led to the introduction of the Van Diemen's Land Postal Act 1828, resulting in the post office becoming a full government department in 1832. By then, regular services were operating across the island, while in Hobart Town itself, mail was being delivered between five and six o'clock each evening, six nights a week. By this time, too, at the instigation of the colony's second postmaster, James Mitchell, Van Diemen's Land had been enjoying its own direct mail service to England, a journey taking 225 days, for more than a decade.

❋

By the late 1840s, the graceful tall ships were looking positively leaden compared to the smart new clippers, which soon slashed by more than half the time it took for the English mail to reach Australian shores. A breakneck non-stop voyage from Liverpool to Melbourne, which had been officially declared a port in 1839, allowing ships to bypass Sydney and sail there directly from England, was now taking as little as three months. Competition to set new records between the clippers was hectic. After setting sail from Southampton on 23 April 1849, the *Phoenician* arrived in Sydney just 91 days later. On her 1852 maiden voyage from Mersey to Melbourne, the *Marco Polo* forged a new record with a 68-day run. *Thermopylae*'s 63-day bolt in 1868 remains an unbroken sail-only record to this day.

Auxiliary steamers, with their engines reserved for when the winds were adverse, took up the brisk pace, using the Great Circle route via treacherous and icy Antarctic waters. Travelling 8 nautical miles an hour via the Cape of Good Hope, the steamers not only dramatically reduced the passage time from England to Australia; with the vagaries of the weather no longer a major impediment, reliable schedules were able to be set for the first time, reducing the cost of carrying both the mails and passengers. Constant breakthroughs in maritime technology throughout this era enabled services to improve rapidly. By the 1890s, the voyage was taking about a month, comparable to what the great ocean liners would achieve in the next century.

Up until the 1830s, all mail had been carried on government-chartered vessels under an exclusive agreement with the East India Company, a shipping giant whose monopolistic practices had sparked Massachusetts Bay's Boston Tea Party some 50 years earlier, an event which would serve as a catalyst to the American War of Independence. But as the might of the industrial revolution gathered pace, the British Government came under increasing pressure from competitive capitalistic forces, and in 1833 began awarding contracts to ships for individual voyages. Meanwhile, the British Admiralty was still obliged to carry the mails whenever one of its ships was ordered to haul a fresh supply of food, building materials and convicts to the Australian colonies.

With news in late 1851 of the discovery of gold, however, it soon became clear to the British Government that the Australian colonies might actually possess considerable commercial value, rather than merely serve as a convenient release valve on the empire's pressure-cooker penal system. The first tenders for a mail steamer service to Australia were called for, signalling the beginning of what would prove to be a century-long battle for antipodean business on the high seas between the Peninsular and Oriental Steam Navigation Company (P&O) and its principal rival, the Orient Steam Navigation Company.

Britain planned for the successful tenderer to operate the Australian leg of the journey as an extension of existing services to Hong Kong and Shanghai, with a steamer connection point in Singapore taking the mail on to Sydney every two months. Ports of call along the way were to include King George Sound, Adelaide and Melbourne. The successful tenderer was P&O, and the company immediately diverted its new steamship the *Chusan* (named after an island off Shanghai) to Sydney. On 3 August 1852, the *Chusan*, on its maiden voyage, brought Australia's first steamer-delivered mail to Sydney, via King George Sound, Adelaide and Melbourne as planned. The steamer's arrival was greeted in Sydney by cheering crowds, a public ball was held in her honour and guests danced to the 'Chusan Waltz'. The National Library of

Australia's archives hold a copy of the waltz's original sheet music for piano, which carries a lithograph of the *Chusan* by J. Allan on the cover, along with a dedication 'to Captain Henry Down and the officers of the Peninsular and Oriental Steam Navigation Company's steam ship *Chusan*'. She departed with the outbound mail for Shanghai 28 days later, marking the beginning of a regular steamship mail delivery from England, shared between the *Chusan* and her sister ship, the *Shanghai*.

For P&O's proprietors, however, the euphoria of the *Chusan*'s debut in Australia proved short-lived. Two years later, the service had yet to turn a profit. The clipper ships and auxiliary steamers ploughing the seas between England and Australia were still proving swifter and cheaper to operate, and in 1854 the company pulled the service. Fresh tenders were called for and the European and Australian Royal Mail Company won with a daring and logistically astounding route between Sydney and Panama, transferring the mail at the isthmus to connect with the new Panama Railroad, before continuing on by steamer across the Caribbean and the Atlantic. But that ambitious route also proved an economic failure, and in 1856, the British Government was once more calling for tenders.

Although still nursing its bruises from its previous failed venture, P&O secured the contract in 1858, agreeing to haul the Australian mail via Suez, Aden and Ceylon. According to the Australian Heritage Council, this complex route involved engaging a steamer in London to travel to Alexandria, then a rail trip across Egypt to Port Said on the Red Sea.

A steamer would then take the mail on to Galle in Ceylon, stopping at Aden and Bombay on the way. Galle, and later Colombo, 120 kilometres to the port's north, was where the Australian mails were separated from the China and Singapore mails, then shipped across the Indian Ocean to King George Sound (and later Fremantle), Adelaide, Melbourne and finally Sydney. P&O agreed to a guaranteed total transit time of 55 days, and the surprisingly successful route would vary little over many ensuing decades; even the opening of the Suez Canal 11 years after the contract was first signed did not divert the colonies' mail from the agreed route, as transferring the bags to Egypt's train network proved more efficient than hauling them through the slow and costly new canal. Until airmail superseded overseas surface mail in the 1960s, this was to remain the basic mail shipping route between England and Australia.

The monopoly was broken in 1883, however, when the New South Wales Government contracted the Orient Steam Navigation Company to operate an independent mail service from Sydney to London via Melbourne, specifying a transit time of 39 days from the time the ship left Australia. The government's decision to transport the mail by rail from Sydney to meet the Orient's waiting vessels in Melbourne not only saved time; it also provided much-needed revenue for the railway's burgeoning operations.

Peeved at always being the last to receive the overseas mail, the colony of Queensland attempted similar independent contracts throughout the 1880s, utilising a route from Singapore and Indonesia. Jagged reefs and violent cyclones made the route particularly treacherous, however, and after one too many shipwrecks, the colony accepted the fact that its citizens would have to maintain their patience.

P&O's monopoly was never to be reclaimed. In 1888, the British Government decided it too would divide its anti-podean mail contracts between the Peninsular and Oriental Steam Navigation Company and the Orient Steam Navigation Company. One would consume the other almost a century later.

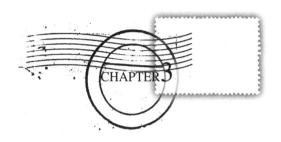

NEWS
FROM EL DORADO

A thimbleful of gold in a waterhole was to radically transform a nation. In 1851, Edward Hammond Hargraves announced to the world the supposed immeasurable riches that lay embedded in the valleys beyond the town of Bathurst, and the Australian gold rush was on. Half the male population of the colony would abandon jobs, land and families and head for the diggings. With word of the 'new California' travelling the globe at lightning speed, the first ships spilt their cargo of British, American, European and Chinese fortune-seekers onto Sydney and Melbourne's teeming wharves just months later. Many of these vessels would depart Australia's shores close to ghost ships, as thousands of seamen also succumbed to the highly infectious gold fever. In the first 12 months, New South Wales would yield 26.4 tonnes of gold, yet this would prove a pittance in comparison to the colony's southern neighbour. Euphoria in the townships of Ballarat and Bendigo followed within months of reports that Bathurst had stumbled over the end of the rainbow, and throughout the decade, the bountiful gold fields of Victoria would account for more than a third of the precious metal's total world production.

The social and economic boom the gold rush brought would hasten the construction of a vast network of railway lines and the laying of thousands of kilometres of telegraph wire across the continent. The discovery would also treble the country's population to 1.7 million in just 20 years, far exceeding the total number of convicts who had landed in Australia over the previous seven decades. Ultimately, the discovery of gold would also signal the end of convict settlement, the British Government soon realising that to continue transportation would effectively supply free passage to future gold diggers, leading them to their possible fortunes.

That the nation's new-found wealth was founded on a piece of skulduggery was only revealed some 40 years later. Hargraves had made no secret of his plans when he first noticed the geographical similarities between parts of inland New South Wales and the Californian gold fields, from which he had recently returned. His intention was to make his fortune by claiming the government reward for discovering gold fields, not by panning them. In the company of retired sea captain-turned-innkeeper John Lister, Hargraves found just five specks of gold in Lewis Ponds Creek on 12 February 1851. Further searches yielded little. Hargraves nonetheless set off for Sydney, leaving Lister, along with William, James and Henry Tom, sons of a local settler, with instructions on Californian panning techniques and the use of a wooden cradle. The party agreed the meagre find should be kept secret. Some weeks later, the brothers and Lister struck gold, about 18 kilometres away from the Tom homestead. William Tom Senior travelled to Sydney and produced a 4-ounce (113-gram) gold nugget to Hargraves. That was the last Lister and the Toms heard of the nugget, until Hargraves announced in The *Sydney Morning Herald* on 15 May that he had discovered gold. A later government report would conclude that this declaration had prompted 'a new era and the commencement of the sudden and marvellous increase in the value of all kinds of property and of the great strides in progress which the Colonies have since made'. Hargraves named the gold field Ophir, a grandiose reference to the biblical city from which King Solomon had legendarily received regular shipments of gold, silver, sandalwood, precious stones, ivory, apes and peacocks. In return, the colony of New South Wales bestowed on Hargraves a gratuity of £10,000, made him a commissioner of crown lands for the gold districts, and upon his retirement, paid him a pension of £250 per annum.

James Tom and John Lister were to spend the next four decades fighting for recognition and compensation for their find which transformed a country. On 25 August 1891, a Select Committee was formed 'to inquire into and report upon the claims (if any) of William Tom, James Tom, and J.H.A. Lister for remuneration as the first discoverers of gold in Australia'. The committee's report presented to the Legislative Assembly two weeks later concluded:

> Although Mr. E.H. Hargraves is entitled to the credit of
> having taught the claimants, Messrs. W. and J. Tom and
> Lister, the use of the dish and cradle, and otherwise the
> proper methods of searching for gold . . . your Committee
> are satisfied that Messrs. Tom and Lister were undoubtedly
> the first discoverers of gold obtained in Australia in payable
> quantity.

The committee was satisfied that Hargraves had 'appeared
to have abandoned the search for gold after his first course of
prospecting with Messrs. Tom and Lister, until they informed
him that they had found 4 ounces of gold, which, according to
his own evidence, they discovered when he was not within
100 miles [160 kilometres] of them'. It was a hollow victory
for the unrecognised pioneers. John Lister had died during the
Select Committee's inquiry, before he had even been given a
chance to present his evidence.

The irony of the whole dispute between Hargraves, Lister
and the Toms is that none of them had in fact discovered
Australia's first gold deposits. Some 28 years prior to their
find, James McBrien, a government surveyor, had found
traces of gold near Bathurst, but his findings were hushed
up by the government for fear of anarchy. Then in 1839 the
Polish explorer Paul Edmund Strzelecki reported sightings
to Governor George Gipps of gold and silver deposits in the
Wellington region. Once again, suppression was the order.
Gipps, the son of an English clergyman, feared the findings
would spark mayhem in a colony where felons still outnumbered the upholders of the law. Two years later, the geologist
Reverend William Branwhite Clarke found a gold nugget near

Cox's River west of the Blue Mountains, but upon showing it to Gipps, the governor reportedly replied: 'Put it away, Mr Clarke or we shall all have our throats cut.' Similar fears were no doubt on the mind of Thomas Hewitt, a merchant and explorer, who forwarded a letter to Melbourne's *Argus* on 26 May 1851:

> Sir, in addition to the already discovered gold fields of Bathurst, I can assure you that I myself have seen to men who have been up in our ranges, and showed me a parcel of gold dust, as far as I could judge, of a very good quality, and they told me that they had been up in the ranges for two months and had done very well by their trip. I have had some little experience in geology . . . but I hope for the good of the country that no such diggings may be made in our part as although through false representation as idle and worthless population might be drawn to the locality, it might at the same time decline many of our steady worthy labourers, who might thrive at the rate at about ten in a hundred. Hoping that this may not be the case. I am, Sir, yours truly, Thos. Hewitt.

Hewitt's hopes were of course dashed. New South Wales' fears of an exodus of yet more workers wasn't helped by Victoria, with that colonial government's promise of a £200 reward for any gold found within 200 miles (320 kilometres) of Melbourne. They came from everywhere, prospectors seeking their fortunes. About 1000 fortune-seekers had converged on Ophir within four months of Hargraves's 1851 announcement. The following year, however, almost 60 ships docked in

Melbourne alone; in a single month American newspapers were full of tales of the new California, in a colony which had only separated from New South Wales a matter of weeks earlier. The *New York Herald* ran articles about American miners amassing instant fortunes. The Melbourne banks were in a spin, the reports claimed, because the gold was coming in so fast, it was impossible to calculate the revenue, let alone the interest owing.

Lucy Ann Hart, the 27-year-old daughter of a stonemason, had been a domestic servant in England before she fled to the Victorian gold fields with her husband in late 1851. In May 1852, she wrote:

My Dear Mother Brothers and Sister, I scarcely know how to excuse myself of how to apologise for my long silence. . . . Now mind Mother, this is the real truth, you may show this letter to any person in the world. This is a second California. Any person can do well here if they like to try. I only wish I could persuade you to come with all the children . . . Should I be so well off in England NO! Work hard and be half starved. Australia is the place to live. I would not come back to England again unless I had enough to keep me without work on no account neither would my husband . . . Why not come Mother? There was many older women than you came out in our vessel and are now doing well . . . Now I shall expect some of you out here in about twelve month from this time.

Lucy's mother never received the enthusiastic advice. She died before the letter reached England.

Reports of a land of milk and honey and promises of untold fortunes there for the taking belied the reality of many desperate prospectors. Women were dying in childbirth, babies were dying of dysentery, and the mud and contaminated water claimed the lives of many.

Desperate to go home to Canada—yet no doubt under the grim realisation his own return would take as long as a letter—Alex Smith gave a more sober appraisal of the gamble that was a career in the Victorian gold fields:

Dear Uncle, I fully expect that after this long silence of years you will have given up all thoughts of ever hearing from me again and I will be thinking I have forgotten you all in Canada but I assure you that is not the case for I am always thinking of you and Anne . . . I am now working digging and made but a poor hand of it and getting tired of it. I have at one time done pretty well, at another as bad, for it is not all gold here, I assure you. I am now making from £1 to 2 and sometimes 10 to 15 . . . per day but how long this may last is uncertain. It is all home work I have made up my mind to leave this as soon as I can muster £200 or even to have £100 clear when I get to Canada for I begin to feel very anxious to hear from you and Anne. I do not know what she has been thinking about my want of correspondence but I am always thinking I would be [there] as soon as a letter.

Not everyone who flocked to Ballarat was searching for gold. In 1851, a report warned Governor Charles La Trobe that 'the postmaster apprehends an entire disruption of the business of his Department, unless remedial measures can be taken'. Somewhat predictably, the deluge of diggers converging on the gold fields was followed by an avalanche of mail. 'The work is day and night,' protested Ballarat's postmaster, as his seniors moved to hike substantially all its employees' salaries. It was a desperate attempt to discourage them from abandoning their jobs and joining the exodus to the gold fields.

David Watson, the son of a Scottish clergyman, was one of the first postal workers sent to the gold fields. He discovered that a job as a post office clerk in the diggings could help him to save more than half his salary each year. He wrote optimistically to his family in Scotland in 1852:

> You will be very much surprised at me when I say that I am very likely to go to the diggings . . . not however, as a digger, but as a Post Office Clerk. I have been promised such a situation from the Postmaster General, with a salary of £200, with lodgings and rations . . .

Watson was just 17 years old when he headed to the diggings. When he got there, he found that his office was nothing more than a tent. The tent was in tatters. Open at both ends, the structure became a wind tunnel, and nowhere in Victoria did the wind bite quite as hard as in Ballarat. Sudden icy gusts would sweep the mail out of the ragged makeshift erection and, as the *Geelong Advertiser* put it, 'distributed [it] to a grateful crowd'. Watson stayed just eight months, earning the equivalent of $16,000 in today's money.

Long before the days of mechanisation, the Ballarat mail workers in that wretched tent processed 1.5 million items by hand in 1852 alone. A *Ballarat Courier* editorial summed it up nicely two years later, suggesting the tattered post office tent 'would make a splendid bonfire'. The postal services were promptly relocated to a bluestone building on the corner of Sturt and Lydiard streets where the present Ballarat Post Office, built 20 years later, stands today.

Haulage to the gold fields was a nightmare. In winter, there were few passable roads, horse-drawn wagons became bogged regularly, and supplies and mail were constantly delayed. Even when the roads were in tolerable condition, the coaches imported to the colonies—designed for the paved and cobbled streets of England—jolted violently on their steel-spring suspensions. Rough colonial road transport was about to undergo a radical make-over, however, with the arrival of a gentleman called Freeman Cobb. Fresh from his entrepreneurial success in America, Cobb arrived in Port Phillip in April 1853, and took less than a month to establish the offices of his haulage company on the corner of Collins and Queen streets. But he soon realised that the poor quality of the colony's roads would spell financial suicide for anyone seeking to run a haulage business to the gold fields. Cobb set about converting his wagons to passenger vehicles, complete with scarlet and gold paint work, floral details, festive yellow wheels and cushioned seats.

Cobb had seen for himself how a radical overhaul of coach design had given the Americans a mode of transport more suited to the rough conditions of the frontier. And Australian road conditions appeared similar to those in the American west. Consequently, the company imported its first Concord coach from the United States the following year. A later model of the Concord stands in the National Museum of Australia today, where she is regarded by staff as something of a screen goddess. The coach featured in the 1920 silent bushranger film *The Man from Kangaroo*, which starred the Australian boxer and all-round sportsman of the 1920s and 1930s Snowy Baker.

According to the museum, it was the Concord's thorough brace suspension, which used thick bullock-hide leather straps, that afforded its passengers a more luxurious coaching experience. The flexible suspension also lessened the weight on the wheels and put less strain on the horses, important factors for travelling the vast distances of the frontier. The very nature of the suspension, however, caused the coach to sway and roll incessantly, giving many a passenger the distinct feeling of becoming seasick.

The pitiable experience of travelling in a Concord was recounted by a 19th-century Englishwoman called Clara Aspinall, whose book *Three Years in Melbourne* was described upon its publication in 1862 as 'a vivacious and very feminine account of her visit to Australia':

But oh! The crushing, the misery, the suffocation of these public conveyances! I am sure that a journey on a penny-a-mile Government train from London to Edinburgh would be the very refinement of luxury as compared with a journey of thirty miles in Cobb's coach . . . I know that I was condensed into a smaller compass than I could have imagined possible. I occupied a seat with two others. There were three passengers in front of us leaning against a leathern strap, at the same time pressing upon us the pure air which was admitted through the windows. Just as I was ready to faint, a lady who sat next to me actually did so, which even somewhat roused me up, turning my thoughts from my own misery—and so I rallied.

Cobb & Co's tariffs weren't cheap either. The fare from Melbourne to Bendigo was £7 each way—today's equivalent of a return business-class airline ticket from Sydney to Melbourne, and well beyond the reach of many a hopeful prospector who earnt as much in a month. Competition between passenger coach companies was fierce. The fare from Parramatta to Penrith, for example, could range from 5 shillings to 10, depending on the number of companies competing on the route. The reputation for speed, rather than comfort, could give any company the leading edge. In *Wild Ride*, a lively account of the rise and fall of Cobb & Co, Sam Everingham tells the story of two rival coaching firms engaging in what was possibly one of the earliest cases of 'hooning' in Sydney's western suburbs. At a galloping pace the packed Kendall coach overtook its equally packed rival Perry coach while approaching a bridge en route to Parramatta. At frightening speed the coaches collided at the mouth of the bridge, smashing the structure's side rails. The Kendall horses plunged into the chasm. Miraculously, neither man nor beast was killed.

Freeman Cobb and his partners began their first carrying service from Melbourne to Port Melbourne in 1853, and made the first scheduled coach run from Melbourne to the Bendigo gold fields the following year. The Concord's speed and ability to handle the rough terrain allowed the company to quickly build a reputation based on reliability. Cobb & Co religiously adhered to its advertised schedules, rather than holding off departures until all seats were filled on a route, as was common practice. Depots were set up every 10 miles (16 kilometres) on the routes, with fresh horses ready and waiting. And a sober driver—something up until then had been far from guaranteed within the coach-driving fraternity—was assured, with a liquor ban for all Cobb & Co drivers on shift. Cobb knew it was the mail contracts that were the big earners for coaching companies and the government would only award contracts to reliable firms. Holding up the mail attracted stiff penalties, given that government offices relied on an efficient post more than anyone. Provisions for fines of up to 10 shillings for every 10 minutes a coach went over schedule were not uncommon in government mail contracts, and passengers accepted with stoicism the fact that their comfort and welfare came second to ensuring the mail ran to schedule.

After almost three years of operation and a respectable share of the passenger market, Cobb & Co had failed to secure a single government mail contract. Moreover, the company was struggling to stay one step ahead of the ever-expanding railways. The Victorian Government saw trains as the transport mode of the future and gave laying tracks priority over building roads. In May 1856, Cobb and his partners decided to call it a day. The company was to change hands three more times before a consortium led by the runtish son of an American farmer—a young man with a fearsome temper and a canny instinct for risk-taking—was to take Cobb & Co into Australian transport history.

James Rutherford and his partners knew instantly that if their £23,000 investment was to pay off, it was the government mail contracts they needed to secure. Yet the business they had bought had only a few paltry mail runs to its name. As it turned out, it was the cricket which would give them the break they desperately needed.

Towards the end of 1861, Australian society was abuzz with preparations for the first tour of the English cricket team. And it was Cobb & Co which won the tender to provide transport for the venerated sportsmen, largely thanks to the existence of a white elephant which had been mothballed only a year earlier.

The *Leviathan* was a mother of a coach, with the capacity to haul more than 60 passengers (with separate compartments for ladies and gentlemen, of course), plus accompanying luggage and mail on the Ballarat to Melbourne route. It was the largest horse-drawn coach ever built in Australia—almost 5.5 metres long and weighing in at 5 tonnes when full. It required a team of up to 16 horses, controlled by reins of more than 30 metres. The *Leviathan* was impractical and, some argued, downright cruel, with many drivers dubbing it the 'Horse Killer'. But it was the perfect grand vehicle to convey a team of English cricketers around the country. On New Year's Day, 1862, the *Leviathan* rolled on to the Melbourne Cricket Ground, amid wild waving and cheering from the appreciative crowd. And the passengers who alighted attracted almost as much adulation as the man who commanded the coach—the inimitable Mr Devine.

In his book, Sam Everingham compares the status of the early coach drivers to the Schumachers, Villeneuves and

Andrettis of modern times. Like Formula One stars, they attracted fame and women:

> They charmed their passengers, told a great story and were highly skilled with horses. Some were so accurate with the 12-foot [3.7-metre] thong on their whip that they could cut a cigarette out of a fellow's mouth without the whip touching his nose.

According to one Darling Downs traveller, a ride with John 'Hell-fire Jack' Carpenter was 'a sure cure for a torpid liver' adding that 'the manner in which that driver would tool that vehicle between two trees, knocking the bark off both of them with the boxes on the wheels was amazing'.

But none were as adored as Ned 'Cabbage Tree' Devine —whose nickname had been earned from the broad-brimmed hat he always wore, fashioned from the leaves of the cabbage tree. According to postal legend, the Tasmanian-born horseman took great delight in challenging overseas gentleman visitors to strap themselves in to the seat next to him on his mad dash between Ballarat and Geelong. Local Ballarat historians swear he could cover up to 100 miles (160 kilometres) in 12 hours along hair-raising roads, and loved to inform his invited co-drivers he had kangaroos lined up along the way to take possession of the mails. Whenever he saw a roadside marsupial, he would holler, 'No mail today', and to the white-fisted tourist's astonishment, the startled animal would bound a hasty retreat into the bush. According to local historians, upon reaching Ballarat, 'Cabbage Tree' would wow the townsfolk by driving his coach 'across a broad ditch at full gallop and, at the end of his journey, hurtle down Main Street still at full gallop, turning sharply into the stable-yard with only inches to spare'.

The ladies loved the charming 'long-legged, sharp-featured, greasy-hatted' larrikin who 'never neglected his cups'. His popularity made him the constant target of poachers from rival firms. Cobb & Co was obliged to secure his loyalty with a £17 per week salary to convince him to continue driving its busiest route, from Geelong to Ballarat. On today's scale that would be a salary of about $70,000, with all living expenses taken care of.

The Australian cricketers may have been thoroughly thrashed by the English that New Year's Day, but the appreciation for the services of the triumphant team's chauffeur was publicly acknowledged with a purse of 300 sovereigns, a gift from the tour's sponsors, the catering firm Spiers and Pond.

Devine died destitute in Ballarat in 1908, yet his large tombstone, erected by his colleagues and ornately decorated with a horse's head, horseshoes and a tiny Cobb & Co coach, bears the words 'peerless driver of Cobb & Co's mail coach'.

The publicity generated from the touring cricketers brought Cobb & Co to the attention of the Victorian Government, and the mail contracts came in thick and fast. By 1870, the company held a monopoly in the colony, and across the country some 6000 Cobb & Co horses were pulling the mail across distances totalling 45,000 kilometres a week.

With news of fresh gold discoveries in New South Wales, James Rutherford's attentions turned north in 1862. In New

South Wales, about 80 per cent of the 300-odd mail contracts covering more than 2000 kilometres were still being serviced by a single rider, and they were often the only connection between each remote settlement. Rutherford knew that to win mail contracts, connections needed to be made with the local politicians and bureaucrats of New South Wales. So on 3 June 1862, a heavily armed caravan of eight Cobb & Co coaches and two wagons headed north to Bathurst, with the goal of making the town its new headquarters. North of Cowra, however, the relocating company passed an even more lucrative operation. The party encountered 'five or six horseman coming towards them' and one led a packhorse 'so heavily loaded as to attract attention'. In Everingham's account of the incident the leader of the group, 'a fellow with a scar under his left eye, rode up to the foremost coach but said as little as possible "in an evidently disguised tone of voice". He then rode on, peering into each coach carefully in turn, taking his party with him'. It was only later, when the Cobb & Co party reached Bathurst, that they learnt they had passed the notorious posse of Frank Gardiner, Ben Hall and Dan Charters. Carrying the spoils of a record heist on the Forbes to Eugowra line just a few days earlier, Gardiner's packhorse had been laden down with £14,000 worth of gold and notes.

The fresh straw typically laid on the floor of all Cobb & Co's coaches wasn't just for the comfort of passengers. When a bushranger crossed a coach's path, the straw became an ideal place to hide the valuables. Fashioning themselves as modern-day Robin Hoods, the bushrangers enjoyed the respect of many a downtrodden settler, and they often received sustenance and protection from locals as they moved between towns. They were superb horsemen and knew the bush better than any policeman. And although lives, usually those of the police, were regularly lost, etiquette within the bushranger fraternity demanded the coach drivers—along with all ladies of course—remained unharmed.

Australia's colonial history is peppered with apocryphal stories of the bushrangers' exploits. One tale recounts the plight of a group of German musicians on their way from Tenterfield, New South Wales, to Queensland in 1868. They begged Fred 'Thunderbolt' Ward not to rob them, but the bushranger could not be moved in his intentions. Nevertheless, he did give assurances that if he had luck at the forthcoming horseraces, he would pay them back. Thunderbolt swaggered his way about the Tenterfield Races, enjoyed a successful flutter and promptly obtained the address of the musicians' Queensland hotel. He forwarded them their money—with interest, of course.

Just outside of the Tenterfield township today, a sign stands indicating the location of Thunderbolt's hideout. The two caves formed by granite boulders gave the bushranger an ideal vantage point as he waited for the mail coaches to rumble down the north-to-south road.

Diggers anxious to carry their gold back to the banks in town ran a gauntlet of bushrangers littering the path from Bathurst to Sydney. But for many a miner, the shark-like practices of the 'professional' gold buyers on the gold fields made the journey no less risky than staying put. To confound the highway thieves, it became common for people to cut banknotes in half, sending the two halves in separate mail coaches, and leaving the recipients to stick the notes back together at the other end.

By the mid-1860s, the postal service had introduced an innovative idea that was to cut heavily into the bushrangers' core business. Money orders enabled miners to send cash home to their families in the city, and city-dwellers to remit money back to Britain as well as make payments.

Around this time, colonial savings banks also began setting up shop in many post offices. The British example of having savings bank branches in rural post offices where stand-alone banks could not be economically justified was embraced by Victoria, then New South Wales. The Government Savings Bank was administered as a subsection of the New South Wales Postal Department. Western Australia and Tasmania took direct control of their post office savings banks, while Queensland and South Australia had specific postmasters appointed to operate the banking agencies. So central had the postal services' role become to people's daily lives, that by the mid-1860s the position of Postmaster-General had become political, elevated to ministerial status by governments in Victoria, New South Wales and Queensland.

The post office banks could only hold so much gold before it all had to be sent back to Sydney, however. The governments of the gold-rich colonies resigned themselves to the expense of providing police trooper escorts for all the mail coaches.

Meanwhile, a fragile wire was revolutionising how fast news travelled. The telegraph was to prove the bushranger's undoing, and by the 1890s, many a postmaster had become a policeman by proxy, frantically tapping out morse code messages such as 'Hall & Co. chased by Police yesterday direction of Burrowa'. Ned Kelly was only too aware of the telegraph machine's potential, at one point shooting up the Post and Telegraph Office in Jerilderie to prevent news of his gang's latest robbery from spreading.

Trains were rarely held up by bushrangers, a fact James Rutherford well knew as he witnessed the appearance of thousands of kilometres of railway tracks across the country. Nevertheless, within three weeks of the company's arrival in New South Wales, on 26 June 1862, Cobb & Co had secured eight new mail and passenger contracts, worth over £4600 a year, where the trains did not run. And the driven business-man was stopping at nothing, including bribing competing operators, to secure the government contracts. Meanwhile, the government was happy that Cobb & Co showed little interest in competing with its railways. Rutherford knew coaching's ongoing viability rested not in beating the trains, but in operating as a feeder to the new inland railheads, and monopolising the mail contracts the rail lines were to bypass.

By the early 1870s, Cobb & Co had snared half of the mail contracts in New South Wales. Yet its relationship with the government was less than harmonious. Friction between the two reached a critical point in 1874, when the Legislative Assembly agreed to remove the penny surcharge for sending newspapers through the mail. Thousands of old newspapers clogged the mail coaches, many with letters scrawled in the margins. A stand-off between Rutherford and the Postmaster-General was inevitable. The government stood its ground and called for fresh tenders for the mail contracts. Perhaps as irrefutable evidence of Rutherford's own shrewdness, Cobb & Co eventually managed to claw back the majority of its mail runs—and an additional £6500 per year in government grants.

By 1865, the company had expanded to Queensland, quickly securing the Brisbane/Ipswich/Toowoomba run. Cobb & Co's Queensland network would eventually stretch as far as Charleville to the west and north to the Gulf of Carpentaria. But the routes didn't get any easier. Many consisted of nothing more than steep muddy tracks, with drivers forced to attach logs to the back of coaches as dragging devices, to prevent them hurtling roof over wheel on the sheer descents. In 1871, the feted and well-travelled English novelist Anthony Trollope was sufficiently impressed by his Cobb & Co driver's skill on the Maryborough to Brisbane line to write:

> The wonder of the journey was in the badness of the roads and the goodness of the coachmanship. I have been called upon by the work of my life to see much coaching, having been concerned for more than 30 years with the expedition of mails . . . I have now travelled over the Gympie road and I feel certain that not one of my old friends in the box seat—and I had many such friends—would, on being shown the road, have considered it possible that a vehicle with four horses could have been made to travel over it . . . I here pronounce my opinion that the man who drove me from Cobbs Camp to Brisbane was the best driver of four horses I ever saw. Had he been a little less uncouth in his manners, I should have told him what I thought of him.

Rutherford worked alongside the expanding rail network—indeed benefiting from it—for almost 30 years. But his company's decision in 1882 to become a partner in rail was to signal the beginning of the end for Cobb & Co. The company recklessly under-bid five other tenders to complete a 90-kilometre section of the Great Northern Railway between Tamworth and Tenterfield. It was a stretch which had taken the mail coaches two days and nights to cover, such was the difficulty of the terrain. The project ran hopelessly behind time, navvies' wages were cut to recoup losses and a full-scale strike ensued. Then typhoid struck, cutting a deadly swathe through the track workers and their families. The line was completed more than a year after the deadline, and instead of making a profit, Cobb & Co lost £80,000. Plagued by manic highs and lows for most of his life, at this point Rutherford attempted to kill himself.

Severe drought was to compound the company's financial troubles throughout the 1890s. While the government mail contracts were earning £20,000 a year in Queensland, the company's feed bill alone was tipping £30,000. The arrival of the horseless carriage sealed the company's fate. A single man and a truck could now deliver what it took a coach, driver, half a dozen grooms and as many as 50 horses to achieve 50 years earlier. By 1917, Cobb & Co had reluctantly moved with the times, replacing horses with Cadillacs and Hupmobiles on its shorter routes. But the company never recovered from the crippling losses it made on the railways.

Cobb & Co's final mail run, from Yeulba to Surat in 1924, proved the ultimate irony in the demise of the coach. Previous heavy rains had caused the lumbering delivery truck to get bogged. A mothballed coach and a scratch team of horses were called out of retirement to finish the final mail run.

A WIRE TO
CIVILISATION

The gold rush not only brought prosperity, bushrangers, and millions of letters; it also created Australia's first immigration tsunami. The hundreds of thousands of migrant labourers who poured into the country from 1851 onwards would cause the population to explode at a rate far greater than any subsequent immigration incentive, including the Snowy Mountains Scheme and the government's £10 Poms incentive in the decades following World War II. The British made up by far the largest contingent, but there were also shiploads of American, Italian, French, German, Polish and Hungarian migrants. It was the 40,000-odd Chinese miners who flocked to the gold fields, however, who fuelled growing racial intolerance. Those tensions boiled over in 1861, with white miners driving the Chinese from their diggings at Lambing

Flat in central New South Wales during six separate riots over 10 months. The most serious riot occurred on 14 July, when about 2000 European diggers attacked the Chinese. Although no one was believed to have been killed, 250 Chinese miners were seriously injured and most had all their belongings destroyed. Somewhat underplaying the rioters' behaviour as an 'intolerable nuisance', an editorial in the *Sydney Morning Herald* noted:

> No doubt there are numbers who look upon the presence of Chinamen as an evil, but we do not believe that there are many who could sympathise with the unprovoked wrongs which they have suffered, or who would not wish to see brought to condign punishment the men who went miles to attack their camp, inflicted upon them every kind of injury, insult, and in some cases most atrocious cruelties. We differ in our opinions on public questions; but as Englishmen we all detest anarchists as an intolerable nuisance to the quiet and the industrious, and a serious peril to those neighbourhoods in which they riot and plunder.

The notorious events at Lambing Flat caused the area to be renamed Young. The pressure of public opinion against the Chinese caused the New South Wales Government to pass the *Chinese Immigration Restriction and Regulation Act* in late 1861, restricting the numbers of Chinese in the colony and laying the foundations for a White Australia Policy which was to endure for more than a century. Queensland introduced similar restrictions in 1877 and Western Australia followed suit in 1886. A decade later, the debate over Federation heard concerns from Queensland that the colony might be excluded if the 'kanaka' trade did not cease, while in New South Wales and Victoria, politicians declared there would be no place for 'Asiatics' or 'coloureds' in a federated Australia. When the country was plunged into war with Japan in 1941, the Prime Minister, John Curtin, would reinforce the White Australia philosophy, declaring 'this country shall remain forever the home of the descendants of those people who came here in peace in order to establish in the South Seas an outpost of the British race'. And an attempt to purge the country of an influx of non-white refugees after the war prompted the Commonwealth's first Minister for Immigration, Arthur Calwell, to make that unforgettable utterance: 'Two Wongs don't make a white.'

While Calwell's statement, made under parliamentary privilege, is today viewed as the quintessential expression from an era in which the White Australia Policy prevailed, there is a strong possibility the minister may have been misinterpreted. *Hansard* of 2 December 1947 records Calwell saying:

> The question from the honourable member for Balaclava also referred to a Chinese [person], who, according to today's press, has been resident in Australia for twenty years and has been told he must go . . . Speaking generally, I think that there is some claim for him to be regarded as a resident of Australia, and I have no doubt that his certificate [visa] can be extended from time to time as it has been extended in the past. The gentleman's name is Wong. There are many Wongs in the Chinese community, but I have to say—and I am sure

that the honourable member for Balaclava will not mind me doing so—that two Wongs do not make a White.

What few Australians today may be aware of was that the honourable member for Balaclava whom Calwell was addressing was Sir Thomas White, a prominent member of the Liberal Party and consequently one of Calwell's parliamentary enemies. While Calwell was undoubtedly trying to be clever, says historian Peter Cochrane, his remarks may not have been as overtly racist as many have assumed. This is something his supporters have always claimed, arguing that the press chose to report the comment with the 'W' in 'White' in lower case, so that 'white' seemed to be referring to a colour rather than a surname.

Calwell's grandfather would have experienced first-hand the racial tensions which gave birth to the immigration policy Calwell was to so enthusiastically champion almost a century later. His grandson Davis Calwell, the son of an Irish-born Pennsylvanian politician who had died when he and his brother Dan were still young, detailed his adventures in the gold field in letters to the family back in America:

The news from the diggings is of the most exciting character—fortunes are made in single claims. Last week at Ballarat a large bed of gold was struck called the Jeweler's Shop, into which twelve holes were sunk and the earth yielded the enormous value of one to two thousand pounds sterling per superficial foot ... What's the use of much to do about nothing, we voluntarily came here and if gold diggin is hard labor to those unaccustomed to it they can easily raise the means to go home with; Nature has given us a good amount of bone, sinew and health these determine us to stand the storm and gather new strength from every obstacle . . . You may all think we are hard hearted in going so far away but we are young and must do something to give ourselves a start in the world. We have human hearts.

Calwell must have been in the Ballarat gold fields during the early stages of the Eureka Stockade. The steep cost of mining licences (a flat rate of 30 shillings a month), lack of representation in Parliament and the ban on buying land were among the grievances which had simmered among the miners for months. Calwell wrote home in 1854, just before the miners were to make their final stand:

Great changes have taken places in time and things particularly political, since our last letter. The diggers, goaded to desperation by the tyranny of the gold Commission officials & exasperated at the contempt of justice in the decision of the court, took things in their own hands, held a meeting & burnt the Eureka hotel, a digger having been murdered there and the proprietor, a 'lag' discharged by the authorities after a mere form of investigation . . . The military & police force were reinforced to the united number of 1500 strong, with orders to collect it at the point of the bayonet. Several skirmishes took place several were hurt on both sides . . .

Twenty-two diggers and three soldiers were killed in the brief but bloody skirmish on 3 December 1854, and many more were wounded. The miners' leader, an Irish civil engineer with politics in his blood, escaped, but only just. Badly wounded, Peter Lalor had his left arm amputated at the shoulder in the home of a Catholic priest. Apocryphal accounts claim Lalor gained consciousness during the operation and seeing one doctor looking pale with squeamishness, uttered 'Courage! Courage! Take it off!'

Largely through popular support of the rebels' cause, the 13 diggers subsequently charged with treason were acquitted, while Lalor remained in hiding until Governor Charles Hotham backed down and lifted the £200 price on his head. As a representative of Victoria's goldminers, the Irishman went on to serve in Parliament, and the Eureka Stockade went on to inspire political activists and artists. The Eureka Flag remains one of the most recognisable national symbols, and on 3 December each year, like-minded Australians around the country still gather to raise a glass to Lalor, and utter the oath: 'We swear by the Southern Cross to stand truly by each other and fight to defend our rights and liberties.'

Davis Calwell clearly had no intention of making this harsh and volatile land his permanent home, writing to his family in America: 'Luck or not, providence permitting, you will soon see us at home, the firmest supporters of a government, which a knowledge of what the citizens of other nations suffer will help us appreciate.' Then he met Elizabeth Lewis. They had 12 children together, including Arthur Albert, father of the man who, despite the later outcry over Wongs and Whites, would rise to lead the Australian Labor Party throughout the better part of the 1960s.

Society grew around the gold fields, as Calwell discovered. A year after his arrival, he wrote home:

The gold fields have changed in a year from a place of toil and self-degradation, where naught but canvas tents once stood public houses, restaurants, places of amusement and comfortable log-cabins have sprung up—good boarding costs but £2 per week and the digger can spend the evening in one of three theatres or a circus, where talent from all parts of the world challenge criticism; stores and store houses are constantly full of every necessary, and most of all the luxuries of life at reasonable prices . . .

And what talent. The gold fields were an irresistible magnet, even for dancing sensations of international renown. Lola Montez had lived in India and Paris. She had been romantically connected with some of the most famous people of her time, including Franz Liszt, Alexandre Dumas and, most famously, the King of Bavaria, Ludwig I. But in 1848, the Irish-born Montez, whose real name was Elizabeth Rosanna Gilbert, was forced to flee Bavaria, after her lover abdicated in the face of his subjects' growing hostility, thought to have been caused in part by Montez's presence in the palace. She landed on her feet in San Francisco, where she perfected what was to become her infamous Spider Dance.

Arriving in Sydney in 1855, an indignant *Sydney Morning Herald*—which had already earned the nickname 'Granny'—described Montez's Spider Dance as 'the most libertinish and indelicate performance that could be given on the public stage'. Rumours the cigar-smoking exotic dancer was in the habit of 'raising her skirts so high that the audience could see she wore no underclothing at all' appeared to be somewhat exaggerated, but nevertheless prompted the *Argus* to decry her performance at the Theatre Royal in Melbourne, as 'utterly subversive to all ideas of public morality'. She was hounded out of town for licentious behaviour. Undeterred, Montez headed for the Ballarat gold fields in early 1856 and there she found an instant fan club. The miners loved the fiery femme fatale, throwing gold nuggets onto the stage while she danced. And the editor of the *Ballarat Times*, Henry Seekamp, received little public sympathy after Montez took a horsewhip to him, to express her disappointment with the newspaper's critique of her artistic ability.

With shiploads of gold bullion being transported back to Britain, trade between the home country and the colonies was exploding, business investments multiplied rapidly and the economy was thriving. But while the banks were booming, the huge distances still separating the country's population meant the postal services on which the banks had capitalised were still consistently posting losses. The costs of extending postal routes and maintaining mail networks were enormous. Yet there remained universal agreement that nothing should stand in the way of expansion and progress, if the growing colonies were to remain connected with each other and the rest of the world.

※

'Without the means of internal communication no country can advance,' the promoters of the newly formed private Sydney Railway Company proclaimed in 1846. Overland railways had transformed mail freight delivery and passenger travel across Britain and America. Now it was Australia's turn. But it would be another five years before work on the first railway line, from Sydney to Parramatta, would commence, as the company went about the task of securing private investors. The discovery of gold also meant that once started, progress would be slow due to chronic labour shortages. To mark Queen Victoria's birthday on 24 May 1855, a trial passenger train finally left Sydney for the Long Cove viaduct (Lewisham today). Four months later the government took over the project from the struggling Sydney Railway Company and on 26 September 1855, the line was officially opened.

More than 3500 passengers crowded the platforms that day, clutching tickets for the inaugural Sydney to Parramatta service, with scheduled stops at Newtown, Ashfield, Burwood and Homebush. Ticket prices ranged from 2 shillings to 4, depending on the class of carriage. The enormous distinctions in comfort between first-, second- and third-class carriages of the day can still be appreciated, with the colony's Loco-motive No.1 with its carriages intact on display in Sydney's Powerhouse Museum. Designed and built in Newcastle-upon-Tyne by Robert Stephenson & Co., it is thought to be the only engine of its type to have escaped becoming scrap metal. Locomotive No.1 went on to haul passengers and goods between Sydney, Campbelltown, Richmond and Penrith for a further 22 years, clocking up more than 250,000 kilometres in its working lifetime. Upon retirement, the engine languished in the Eveleigh Railway Workshops' 'Rotten Row' for nine years, before being restored and presented to the museum in 1884.

Trains don't sink, although according to the Australian Heritage Council, a New South Wales mail train did once dive into a swollen creek. More importantly, trains were rarely the target of bushrangers. So it was by rail that people quickly came to entrust their mail and bullion. The only serious armed robbery ever recorded on an Australian train took place after the colonial era, in 1930 at Emu Plains, with two masked men relieving the Mudgee mail train of £18,203.

As tracks were constructed and extended throughout the 1860s, the colonies' mail was moving much faster than had previously been possible by land or sea. In 1883, the marvel of overnight interstate mail delivery took place, with the opening of the Melbourne to Sydney line. Until other interstate and coastal lines were completed, however, reliance on tedious sea mail remained a fact of life for many 19th-century Australians. The bulk of mail between Sydney and the north coast of New South Wales was delivered by ship right up until 1923.

With the expansion of the Australian intercolonial railways came a new importance granted to South Australia. The Adelaide General Post Office became the exchange centre for all overseas mail destined for colonies to its east, once the rail line between Melbourne and Adelaide opened in 1887. Designated mail trains which ran from Largs Jetty (near Port Adelaide) to the GPO were always at the ready, waiting for the telegraph message from the lighthouse keeper on Kangaroo Island to signal that the steamer from Colombo had been sighted. The trains would carry the mail to the GPO, where it was sorted then forwarded by mail train to Melbourne. During that journey the Victorian mail was separated from the New South Wales and Queensland mails, and then from Melbourne another mail train would carry the overseas mail on to Albury. At this point, the New South Wales rail services took over, taking the mail on a speedy overnight journey to Sydney in time for the morning post. By the turn of the century, this complex delivery system had become a weekly service. A letter posted in Sydney could reach its Brisbane address the following day, via the mail train to Newcastle and a hasty transfer at Wallangarra. The system was not to change until the completion of the Trans-Australia Railway in 1917, with Port Adelaide relinquishing its role to Fremantle.

The efficient habit of sorting the mail en route began soon after the railways opened, giving rise to the proliferation of Travelling Post Offices (TPOs) throughout the late 1800s. Letters could be posted at a city terminal station right up until the mail train's evening departure. By the time the train reached its destination the following morning, the mail had been sorted and stamped and was ready for delivery. Postal workers operated in specially fitted carriages, working the 'up or down' shift of a two-way journey. It was not uncommon for the postal carriages to have their own letter boxes, so mail could be posted at stops along the line.

The Melbourne to Geelong and Ballarat route pioneered the first TPO in 1865, but it was on the long hauls, such as those in Western Australia, where the TPOs really made a difference in speed and efficiency. By the 1890s, mail from Albany to Perth could take as little as 18 hours—the time it took the mail train to travel between the two points, 390 kilometres apart. No colony relied on the TPO more than New South Wales, however. The practice of sorting the mail in-transit persisted until the mid-1980s, and terminated only when industrial disputes on the railways became so frequent it threatened the reliability of the state's postal services.

71

Australia Post invested in a fleet of trucks and the days of the TPOs were over.

※

When news broke of the bloodshed near Bakery Hill, it travelled faster than any bad news had travelled before. Reports of the Eureka Rebellion were some of the first messages sent by telegraph. The harbinger of the modern e-mail phenomenon, the telegraph was a miracle of 19th-century colonial life.

'We can go to England in as many weeks as then took months, and can communicate in as many minutes as then occupied months,' mused the New South Wales Postmaster-General George Lloyd, upon the intercontinental telegraph's completion in August 1872. Australians were to become the world's greatest users of telegraphic services, sending 35 million telegrams a year by 1946—that's four for every Australian man, woman and child.

News of the great strides American communication technology had made using Samuel Morse's marvellous invention had been filtering into the colonies for almost a decade, before one of the inventor's pupils arrived in Melbourne in 1853. Samuel McGowan hoped to make his fortune providing a communications link between the country's major cities and the gold fields. But the early overtures the Canadian made to potential backers for his private company were soon cut short. The electric telegraph was to be under the control of the colonial postal services, and subsequently the Commonwealth Government, from the very beginning. So McGowan tendered for the Victorian Government contract to build the country's first experimental telegraph line instead.

He won and on 3 March 1854, the first message was sent along a 10-kilometre line between Williamstown and Melbourne. Some 4000 more telegrams were to follow over the next 10 months. The service was clearly viable. Within just a few years, all of Victoria's key regional centres were connected by wire to Melbourne, with Sydney and Adelaide tapping into the system in 1858. The following year a submarine cable under Bass Strait linked Tasmania to the mainland.

By 1870, the telegraph had become an integral part of the postal services, as colonial governments moved to merge the two operations of mail and electric messages. But while the speed of intercolonial communication had improved enormously over this time, messages from abroad were still taking about 40 days. Submarine cables were already threading their way across the Atlantic. Great Britain was linked to Europe, later extending the connection to India, then further south to Singapore. The final leg to the Australian mainland was a mere ditch in comparison. The stumbling block lay not in the construction of the undersea link, but in the overland cable route—and who should build it.

The line would have to pass through a vast and remote interior. The costs would be huge but so too would the benefits to the state which succeeded in receiving the international connection.

The Queensland Government's proposal was to connect the submarine cable at Normanton on the Gulf of Carpentaria, from where messages would go down the line to Brisbane to hook up with the other colonies. The Western Australians were keen to take charge of the submarine cable at Perth, and establish an overland cable across the Nullarbor to Adelaide.

South Australia's proposal seemed the most precarious of all. Encouraged by the diaries of explorer John McDouall Stuart, who had made the only successful south to north crossing of the continent in 1862, Adelaide's Postmaster-General and Superintendent of Telegraphs, Charles Todd, planned a route straight through the country's inhospitable and still largely unknown heart, from Port Augusta to Darwin.

Queensland moved quickly, securing a partnership with the British Australian Telegraph Company which agreed to extend its Singapore cable to Batavia, and then to Darwin. An overland route would then feed the line into the Queensland network. By June 1870, the deal seemed all but sealed. But at the 11th hour, the South Australian Government sped through legislation in both houses of Parliament committing the necessary funds to build the line to Darwin via a different route in just 18 months. The South Australian Government had agreed to finance the entire project. Queensland's route may have been easier, but South Australia's offer to pick up the entire tab for the connection secured the contract.

Todd called for tenders for the construction of the Overland Telegraph Line, and prepared for the task of laying a thin wire across 3200 kilometres of desert, bush and rock. The line was divided into three sections, with the private firms E.M. Bagot and Derwent & Dalwood winning the contracts for the southern and northern sections respectively. That left the most challenging central section between Macumba River and Tennant Creek to Todd himself. Unlike in the other colonies, the Postmaster-General in South Australia was a bureaucratic position, not political, which may have given Todd greater freedom in realising his vision. It was to be an adventure the 44-year-old mathematician and former Cambridge University astronomer could never have anticipated 15 years earlier, when he first arrived in Australia.

The Overland Telegraph Line produced an economic mini-boom in itself, giving employment to hundreds of labourers, tradesmen, surveyors and linesmen over its two-year construction phase. With the gold fields of Victoria and New South Wales nearing depletion, and subsequent finds in Queensland's Canoona and Gympie showing significantly less promise of instant wealth, there were none of the labour shortages that had plagued the progress of the railways' construction 20 years earlier. It would be another seven years before gold was discovered in Beaconsfield, Tasmania, while the rushes in Kalgoorlie and Coolgardie in Western Australia were still another two decades away.

In little more than two months after the contract was signed, Adelaide's timber yards had produced 30,000 ironbark insulator pins and steamers had hauled thousands of wrought-iron poles from the other side of the world. Accompanied by 400 bullocks, teams of draughthorses and packhorses and two camel trains, a workforce of more than 500 then headed for the interior. A party of surveyors had been dispatched several weeks earlier, with little more to guide them than the notes in Stuart's diaries.

In Marcella Hunter's account of the line's construction, she describes the challenges the working party faced:

Although well equipped, nothing could prepare the work teams for the gruelling conditions ahead as the line passed over stony deserts, harsh scrubland, huge gibber plains, towering sandhills and tropical swamps. Despite searing heat at times, the men pushed on, even when their tools became too hot to handle. Hundreds of wooden telegraph poles cut from trees found in the locality—particularly eucalyptus—were erected. When timber was scarce, the imported wrought-iron poles that the bullock teams had hauled from Adelaide were used. Altogether, around 36,000 poles and 60,000 insulators were used to build the line. However, white ants gnawed their way through many of the poles, requiring their complete replacement some 10 years later in the 1880s.

The local indigenous tribes encountered along the way observed the commotion with bemusement. From the debris left in the construction's wake the locals fashioned knives, scrapers, fish hooks, axe-heads and spear tips, innovations the rear work party noted as it followed, threading the wire from pole to pole. As the electrical currents were made and test messages sent down the line, the Aborigines wondered at the 'singing wire'. Across all three sections of the line, 11 repeater stations about 200 kilometres apart would be built. A nearby water source was a prime factor in choosing the location of each station, which stretched from Port Augusta in the south to Yam Creek in the Northern Territory, which at this stage was administered by South Australia. Gold had been discovered at Yam Creek in December 1870. History would show that the state which opened up the interior at huge financial cost would be the only state not to benefit from a gold rush of some nature.

By the appointed deadline, the cable running from Darwin to Banjoewangie in West Java had already been finished. But the overland line was running over budget and hopelessly late, plagued by heavy rain in the northern sector and dust storms in the centre. Todd pressed on, taking over the top section in the final months of construction, and on 22 August 1872, the final join was made at Frew's Ironstone Pond. The first test message was then wired back by Todd to Adelaide, more than 3000 kilometres away: 'We have this day, within two years, completed a line of communications two thousand miles long through the very centre of Australia, until a few years ago a terra incognita believed to be a desert.'

Upon receiving the news, a jubilant South Australian Government declared a half-day holiday and there were celebrations in the street. The venture had made a hero out of Todd, who received congratulatory messages from prominent business people and politicians throughout the country and overseas ambassadors. He would go on to become a knight of the realm, and, through the Todd Committee, become an indispensable force in reforming and integrating the country's telecommunications systems in the lead up to Federation. Throughout this time, he remained Postmaster-General and Superintendent of Telegraphs, only retiring from the job five years before his death, at the age of 84. The Todd River was named in his honour, while Alice Springs, one of the towns which owed its birth to Sir Charles Todd's overland telegraph wire, was named after his wife. With a regional population of around 39,000 today, Alice Springs is the heartland of central Australia's pastoral industries. As settlements had organically sprung up wherever a Cobb & Co coach stopped for the night, so too would the repeater stations give birth to the towns of Beltana, Strangways Springs, The Peake, Charlotte Waters, Barrow Creek, Tennant Creek, Powell Creek, and Daly Waters.

For Australians living in the 1870s, the opening of the Overland Telegraph Line had an enormous impact on their lives and work. Overnight, news from the other side of the world would reach the colonies within a matter of hours instead of weeks. It proved a boon to the country's newspapers, with the *Sydney Morning Herald* labelling the overland telegraph 'a great instrument of modern civilisation'. In the final four months of the telegraph's maiden year, Australians would be reading about the Great Boston Fire, the victory of Ulysses S. Grant in the United States presidential election, and the eerie discovery of the crewless *Mary Celeste*—all within 24 hours of these events' occurrence.

At £239,588, the Overland Telegraph Line had cost twice its original estimate to build and the South Australian Government had picked up the entire bill. Initially, the line's services did not come cheap to the public either, with a 20-letter telegram to England costing £9—the equivalent of a day's wage per word. Over the better part of the next century, however, that cost to send a word down the line would gradually diminish to a comparatively trifling shilling. With the deaths of just six men, the cost to human life during construction was surprisingly low, given the working conditions and the extremes of the natural environment the workers battled against. And the telegraph would go on to save innumerable lives, as the Reverend John Flynn was to learn some 40 years later.

One of the most gripping tales demonstrating the vital role the telegraph could play in people's lives is the story of Darcy the stockman. Jimmy Darcy was mustering cattle on the Ruby Plains Station in the Kimberley, 75 kilometres south of Halls Creek, when he was thrown from his horse. A 12-hour, 65-kilometre buggy ride brought the barely conscious Darcy to Halls Creek Post Office, the logical place one would take a wounded man in a town with no doctor or hospital. The local postmaster, Fred 'Doc' Tuckett, was the closest thing to a medico the town had, and just one look at Darcy was enough for Tuckett to start frantically wiring for the closest doctors, one 400 kilometres away, the other more than 600 kilometres. Both were uncontactable. According to the transcripts later published in Flynn's church magazine *The Inlander*, Tuckett administered morphine then set about trying to contact a Dr J.J. Holland, who had taught the postmaster most of his rudimentary medical knowledge during a St John Ambulance course. Tuckett telegraphed Perth GPO and Dr Holland was summoned. Under special authority, the wires were freed, the 'line clear' signal given, and a tortuous conversation in morse code between two men linked only by a single 3674-kilometre strand of wire began. It was soon established that Darcy had a ruptured bladder.

> *Tuckett: 'Operate?'*
> *Holland: 'Yes you must.'*
> *Tuckett: 'No instruments.'*
> *Holland: 'Penknife and razor.'*
> *Tuckett: 'No drugs.'*
> *Holland: 'Permanganate of potash.'*

Tuckett: 'I can't do it.'
Holland: 'You must.'
Tuckett: 'I'll kill the man.'
Holland: 'If you don't hurry, the patient will die anyway.'

Darcy was strapped to a makeshift operating table and so began a seven-hour procedure dictated by morse code down the line from Perth. The operation on the conscious Darcy was performed by Tuckett without a slip, and the stockman survived the night. A day later, however, complications set in. As *The Inlander* reported:

The injury proved to be of no ordinary character, and although two subsequent operations were performed under similar conditions, it became evident that only a medical expert could undertake this case for permanent cure. After consultation with colleagues, the city specialist (Dr Holland) decided that the risk of bringing the patient to him was too great. So there was only one way out—he himself must travel up over 2000 miles. Maybe the man could last out till he arrived.

Dr Holland embarked on a journey, first by cattle boat, then Model-T Ford, horse and sulky, and finally on foot. At dawn on the 12th day, he arrived at Halls Creek Post Office.

'How is the patient, Mr Tuckett?'
   'He died yesterday.'
   The doctor examined the still form. He was able to say that the operation had been well and skilfully performed and had

been completely successful as far as they could go; but malaria had cut in while they waited, and the spent strength then ebbed out. As it was in the beginning. The pioneer's way. Pay with courage, pay with toil, pay with simple sacrifice of three-fourth of necessary comforts; pay with life they should seldom be permitted to give. Is providence to blame? Some men will say so. Most of us will be mute; pause to ponder further—and look nearer.

Jimmy Darcy's agonising ordeal and subsequent death was not utterly in vain. An entire nation had been gripped by his struggle, through Rev. John Flynn's publication of the above description. And a determined Flynn would go on to establish Queensland's Aerial Medical Service, which later became the Royal Flying Doctor Service of Australia.

Throughout the last decades of the 19th century and into the 20th century, a landscape of criss-crossing wires linking a country's population became a familiar sight. Over a 20-year period from 1901, the length of pole routes linking the country to the electric telegraph increased from 160,000 to 240,000 kilometres, and the number of telegrams lodged per year rose from just under eight million to almost 18 million.

As the *Argus* had pointed out a half-century earlier, the telegraph was indeed 'the most perfect invention'.

GROWING PAINS

*The Fizzer was due at sun-down, and at sun-down a puff of dust
rose on the track, and as a cry of 'mail oh!' went up all round
the homestead, the Fizzer rode out of the dust . . . In half a mo'
the seals were broken, and the mail-matter shaken out on the
ground. A cascade of papers, magazines, and books, with a fat,
firm little packet of letters among them.*
JEANNIE GUNN, WE OF THE NEVER-NEVER

There was a saying about Henry Packham, the Katherine to
Powells Creek mailman more famously known as 'the Fizzer'.
One could never be quite sure whether the Fizzer arrived at
sun-down, or the sun went down when the Fizzer arrived.
Packham's 'never a day late and rarely an hour' reputation
was legendary in the Northern Territory at the turn of the
19th century—and extraordinary, given his mail route was
1600 kilometres long. Immortalised in Jeannie Gunn's 1908
book *We of the Never-Never*, the Fizzer earned his moniker

through his fondness for saying it 'took a bit of fizzing' to equip himself for the long, lonely trek his £200-a-year contract demanded he make every six weeks. It was assumed the Adelaide-born former stockman from Renner Springs possessed an in-built compass, so adept were he and his pack-horse at negotiating the vast Northern Territory outback with its scattering of spare isolated homesteads, including Elsey Station where Gunn wrote her memoir.

Such outback postmen may have come from sturdy stock, but getting the mail through could sometimes be lethal. Packham had inherited the Katherine to Powells Creek mail run from Fred Stibe, who had died of thirst on the job during the 1902 drought. The Fizzer too would perish in the line of duty, drowning as he attempted to cross the flooded Dashwood Crossing at Campbells Creek. On a mercy dash from Victoria River Downs Station, he was desperately trying to deliver a message seeking medical help for a woman on the station who had fallen seriously ill.

It was mail routes like Packham's that had contributed to the failure of the colonies' postal services to break even. The long routes were time-consuming and expensive, even when private contractors were used whose multi-purpose transport services included hauling the mail. As the country moved towards Federation, isolated communities in a sprawling land expressed fears their links to the outside world would be rationalised, once under the control of a single, monolithic postal service.

The merging of six colonial post, telegraph and telephone departments into one—fittingly headquartered in the country's new capital, Melbourne—meant mailmen like Packham would become public servants under a new Commonwealth Government. The essential role the postal services had played over the course of the 19th century was not lost on the fathers of Federation, who began debating the issue at the first Australian Federation Conference in 1890. The 'means of communication carried in all directions constituted one of the major reasons for the union of the colonies', Sir Henry Parkes enounced in his opening address, and it was agreed by all that a uniform postal system would be essential in a united Australia. It was a former Victorian Cobb & Co employee, Alfred Deakin, who officially proposed at the conference that all of the colony's post, telegraph 'and other like services', along with the entirety of assets, be ceded to the new Federal Government which was scheduled to be established on 1 January 1901.

The Commonwealth Postmaster-General's Office, located between Melbourne's Spring Street and Flinders Lane, opened for business just two months later. It was quickly to become known by the less weighty name of the PMG's Department, and under this title, the government body was to administer the nation's entire postal, telegraph and telephone services for the next 74 years.

In keeping with the usual practice of the former colonies, the inaugural Commonwealth Postmaster-General was a cabinet position. Western Australia's Sir John Forrest did not last long, however. The sudden death of the Minister of Defence, James Dickson, just 17 days after his appointment led to the first cabinet reshuffle by an Australian Federal Government. Forrest moved portfolios, and turned his mind to integrating the six colonial forces into a unified

Commonwealth Military Force. He went on to serve as treasurer in five ministries.

Prime Minister Edmund Barton handed the Commonwealth Postmaster-General's position to Queensland's former Postmaster-General, James Drake, a senator *Melbourne Punch* magazine described as 'a plodder—thorough rather than brilliant', with 'a sense of humour, a gift of portraiture, a good memory and a thorough knowledge of English literature'. Drake was also known for his antipathy towards Asian immigration, his opinions frequently being aired in the weekly publication *Boomerang*. Drake had co-edited the magazine with William Lane some seven years before the latter migrated to Paraguay in 1894 to form his ill-fated Australian utopia.

Four months after the PMG's Department began its official operations, Drake named Robert Townley Scott as the senior public servant who would head the department. Scott was a fellow Queenslander, and his appointment as Secretary drew criticism of state bias, which did not bode well for a behemoth organisation taking its first baby steps. Scott was nonetheless eminently well qualified and experienced, having worked in Queensland's postal services for almost 40 years and rising to the position of Under-Secretary and Superintendent of Telegraphs in 1899.

As Secretary to the PMG's Department, Scott faced a seemingly impossible mission. It was the largest of seven new federal departments, having inherited from the colonies about 10,000 permanent staff, 6000 contractors and over 7000 offices spread throughout the country. Only the New South Wales Government Railways rivalled the new department for sheer scale of enterprise. The department's assets, however, were comparatively poor, with a capital value of just £6 million. With these scant resources, Scott set about navigating his way through six different postal and telegraph acts, six different colonial postal rates and six distinct denominations of colonial postage stamps. It would be more than 10 years before Australia got its first national stamp and uniform postal rates. Consequently, for the first decade after Federation, Victorians continued to enjoy penny postage for their standard letters, while their cousins in New South Wales paid double.

Scott found establishing a central administration to be near impossible and he was hamstrung from the beginning from a number of quarters. Above him he had to defer to the Public Service Commissioner over staffing issues, and to the Department of Home Affairs over expenditure. Below him, power struggles with the colonies' former postmasters-general (now serving as his deputies) were not uncommon. Unity was still a distant goal when the first mutterings about commercialisation were heard. The geographically larger states began to fear their postal services to rural and remote regions would be diminished. This was to be the subject of a recurring debate for three-quarters of a century.

By 1908, the situation had deteriorated to the point the Federal Government was obliged to call a Royal Commission. The commission took two years to investigate every aspect of the postal service's quagmire, and its findings were less than laudatory towards Scott (who, well into his sixties, had had his appointment renewed annually for the past four years) and the successive postmasters-general he had worked under. The cabinet position had changed hands eight times in just nine years.

While the commission concurred with Scott's opinion that his department had been starved of funds and hampered by administrative constraints, it also found there had been a serious lack of accountability. Among the commission's recommendations was an independent board of management, and regular annual reporting. The PMG's Department produced its first annual report the following year.

Scott decided he'd had enough and announced his retirement in December 1910. According to his biographer, Ian Carnell, the man described as a 'kindly disciplinarian . . . nimble of limb and agile of mind' had been given an impossible task. His 'office [had] been to him tennis, cricket, fishing, theatre—even at times church', and his diligence and integrity were widely acknowledged. He was made a Companion of the Imperial Service Order in 1903 and received a knighthood the year before he retired.

For Aeneas and Jeannie Gunn, and the thousands of other families living in the remote stretches of a brown land, at least one of the inquiry's findings would have given them heart. While 'every effort should be made to conduct the services along business lines', the PMG's Department was not a 'purely commercial proposition', the commissioners concluded. They had endorsed a system of cross-subsidisation, ensuring that postal services charged in the cities would continue to cover the more costly but vital services to the bush. The jobs of Henry Packham and his like were safe. And in just four years' time, a young country would need all the courage and dedication of the Fizzer as it prepared for war.

※

World War I would have an effect on the new nation of Australia like no war before or since. Like Eureka just two generations earlier, it became a defining moment in the shaping of a young nation. It started off as a great adventure, says journalist and historian Les Carlyon. It was also the first 'big thing' Australians would collectively do in the world. A nation for just 13 years, the adolescent Australia was yearning to prove itself. It was a war that touched everyone, says Carlyon.

> In Australia there wasn't a single little country hamlet that hadn't seen someone off. Everyone, in one way or another, was touched by the war because in the end we sent 330,000 young Australian men overseas. They were probably the most generous spirits of that generation, in a tiny country that had only become a country in 1901.

Out of a population of 4.9 million, one in three of Australia's eligible men were wounded on the battlefields of Europe and the Middle East, and one in 10—some 60,000—were killed. As many again would die within a decade of the war's end from their enduring wounds, both physical and psychological. Many of those who returned would say that, after their lives, the thing they valued most at the front was the mail. It was the lifeline to home. While researching his books *Gallipoli* and *The Great War* Carlyon found that some of the most poignant photographs he came across were from France and Belgium, depicting groups of Australian soldiers grinning up at the camera, each with a letter clasped in his hand. Invariably, it was the familiar handwriting on an envelope tossed to a soldier which served as the sole morale booster on the battlefront. And the letters they sent home were some of the most evocative in the whole course of Australian history.

'I think the most remarkable thing about those letters from the First World War are that they're evidence of what we might call a golden age of letter writing and it's a golden age that's not going to come back because of things like telephones, internets and text messages,' says Carlyon.

> ...and the standard of literacy in these letters, I think it's a fair comment, is probably higher than standards of literacy today. And that's amazing, given that many of these soldiers would have left school at the age of 13. These blokes were a whole world away from Australia, they left in 1914 and some didn't come back until 1918. The only link to family and everything was the mail.

In 1914, Australia had a literate population for the first time says Bill Gammage, author of *The Broken Years*. And through these letters, the men documented their hopes, fears and emotions as they prayed for the courage to get them through the war. The horrific impact of fighting in battle was rarely communicated back home in any detail, however, showing a remarkable sense of self-censorship and propriety. Lieutenant Eric Chinner was a 22-year-old bombing officer for the 32nd Battalion when he wrote home:

> I am not afraid. Of course I am a bit shakey but not very scared. I'm writing this to you because you will then know

something of what is doing should anything happen. I feel sure God will watch over me and pull me through. Cheerio Anyway.

Chinner perished in a prisoner-of-war camp. Not yet 30, Lieutenant Jacques d'Alpuget, a former Rugby Union international, was killed two days after writing this:

> We are preparing for something big. The biggest move any Australians have done in France. Long before this letter reaches you, you will know the result which I feel certain will be a credit of Australia. If I happen to be one of the unlucky ones you know I have done my best and led a straight life right up to the finish.

Clyde Grenness, a 21-year-old postal worker from Melbourne's Malvern Post Office, served in the Middle East with the 8th Infantry Battalion, then later in Europe on the Western Front. He wrote regularly to his sister Mabel, who he affectionately called Queenie. His letters home were invariably cheerful and light on information, as all correspondence had to pass the field censor to ensure it did not contain specific details of troop movements.

> Lately we had travelled through some beautiful country. You can see for miles in places red poppies growing wild, and to see them peeping just above the green grass it looks very nice. I think Annie J. should make a good school teacher. I guess she will be a great favourite . . . I saw Jack Bromley last Tuesday but it was only for a few seconds. Hardly time to

speak to him. Well Queen I think this is all this time with best love to all, your loving brother, Clyde.

The splendour of those poppies was probably the last thing of beauty Grenness saw. Ten days later, on 26 July 1916, he was killed in action. Queenie received a telegram bearing the news her brother had been killed. A few days later, she received that final sunny letter home. Nobody wanted to see the telegram boy walk through their front gate during those war years.

As was the case with all the country's postal employees, the Postmaster-General had kept Grenness's job open for him. He was one of 4000 postal employees who signed up for service, but not all ended up fighting in the trenches. Those in the Postal Corps, established in 1916, nevertheless found themselves in terrifying surrounds, sorting mail in tents sometimes pitched as close as a couple of kilometres from the front line. 'We received and dispatched mail on the roadside for two days; no shelter overhead . . . up to our knees in mud,' wrote one Postal Corps worker serving in Belgium in 1916.

There was a lot of mail to sort. Millions of items were posted to the front during World War I. About 3.7 billion items passed through the Commonwealth Post Office between 1914 and 1919. There were just 170 letters in a single bag when the Hobart GPO sent its first consignment of mail addressed to troops serving overseas. Two years on, the same post office was dispatching 112 mailbags at a time, all destined for the Australian Imperial Forces. While letters were in the majority by far, other items such as parcels containing basic necessities or a few meagre treats were popular among the diggers at the front, as were newspapers.

As the AIF mail began to bulge from every GPO in the country, the PMG's Department struggled to find enough staff to handle the load. Not only were all the post offices handling unprecedented amounts of mail, they were also handling thousands of pounds in money order remittances to troops overseas, as well as assisting the government in its war loans scheme. The post office also became the repository for letters to thousands of men in the navy. Unsure where a ship might be stationed at any given time, family members at home would address their letters simply with the recipient's name and the vessel they were on, c/o their General Post Office. The Navy Office would keep in regular contact with postal authorities to inform them where the letters were to be redirected.

A notice gazetted at an unknown date highlighted the tyranny of distance families would have felt keenly, with their loved ones on the battlefields on the other side of the world.

The practice of marking a soldier's letter 'Wounded' or 'In Hospital' should be discontinued, as it is a handicap to the Postal Corps. The postal authorities abroad emphasise the fact that in the interval between notification of casualties to people in Australia and the receipt of letters in England, France, or elsewhere, the soldiers in many cases have rejoined their units. Therefore, the original addresses only should be put on the envelope.

As the dreaded letters bearing news of casualties increased and the war dragged on, what started out as a young nation's big adventure turned into an expedition of horror, claiming the lives of tens of thousands of young able-bodied men. Australians were being killed in numbers that today we'd find incomprehensible, says Carlyon. At Fromelle in France, 2000 men died in a single night and there was no question of bringing bodies home.

'It started off as a great adventure and it also started off as the first big thing Australia did in the world, because we'd only been a nation since 1901,' he says. 'And slowly, over about 18 months the realisation came. That wars don't kill hundreds of people, they kill millions, and the gloss went off the adventure.'

By 1917, there were far fewer jaunty letters such as those Queenie cherished from her brother just a year earlier. A 29-year-old Lieutenant R.M. Berry of the 25th Battalion wrote home:

All my pals I came over with are gone, but 7 of our 150 remain, it's simply scientific murder, not war at all. As for seeing Germans it's all lies, you never get close enough to do that, unless in a charge. I keep smiling, but to tell you it takes some doing. The premonition I had when leaving Sydney that I would never see home again still hangs about me. One would be unnatural to go through uninjured, if I get out of it with a leg and arm off I'll be perfectly satisfied, so you will understand what it is like. So don't get married until after the war.

Lieutenant Berry was killed in action on 7 February 1917. A 32-year-old Lieutenant H.W. Crowle of the 10th Battalion died only a few hours after writing his final letter home to his wife and son. It provides a rare and stark glimpse of what death on the battlefield must have been like.

Dearest Beat and Bill, Just a line you must be prepared for the worst to happen any day. It is no use trying to hide things. I am in terrible agony. Had I been brought in at once I had hope. But now gas gangrene has set in and it is so bad that the doctor could not save it by taking it off as it had gone too far and the only hope is that the salts they have put on may drain the gangrene out otherwise there is no hope. The pain is much worse today so the doctor gave me some morphia, which has eased me a little but still is awful. Tomorrow I shall know the worst as the dressing was to be left on for three days and tomorrow is the third day. It smells rotten. I was hit running out to see the other officer who was with me but badly wounded. I ran too far as I was in a hurry and he had passed the word down to return, it kept coming down and there was nothing I could do but go up and see what he meant. I got two machine gun bullets in the thigh, another glanced off by my water bottle and another by the periscope I had in my pocket. You will see that they send my things home. It was during the operations around Mouquet Farm, about 20 days I was in the thick of the attack on Pozieres as I had just about done my duty. Even if I get over it I will never go back to the war as they have taken pounds of flesh out of my buttock. My word they look after us well here. I am in the officer's ward and can get anything I want to eat or drink but I just drink all day changing the drinks as I take a fancy. The stretcher bearers could not get the wounded out any way than over the top and across the open. They had to carry me four miles with a man waving a Red Cross flag in front and the Germans did not open fire on us. Well dearest I have had a rest, the pain is getting worse and worse. I am very sorry dear, but still you will be well provided for I am easy on that score. So cheer up dear I could write on a lot but I am nearly unconscious. Give my love to Dear Bill and yourself, do take care of yourself and him.

Your loving husband, Bert.

The post office had become central to people's lives. Their noticeboards kept local communities everywhere up to date. But not all the news was welcome. Pinned to the boards with grim regularity were the lists of casualties. So it was only fitting that when peace was finally declared on 11 November 1918 and people took to the streets to celebrate, it was to the post office they invariably headed. Tom McGuire, a resident of Traralgon in Victoria at the time, wrote a lively reminiscence of Armistice Day, which has been preserved by the local heritage council.

News of the end of the War to end Wars was first received in Traralgon by Nurse Miller . . . from her sister in Melbourne. Eric Hinde was the telephonist on night duty that night, and I happened along about 9.00 p.m. at the time the call was going through. Central Exchange provided confirmation of the doings in Melbourne and inside two minutes it was 'on' in Traralgon.

The first person I nearly knocked flat in the gutter was Grandpa Wickes, the old chap with a beard to his belt and a Kettle Drum in his hand. He took up a position in front of the Post Office and beat out a rhythm that no doubt caused a stirring of the sleepers at the Bluff. He was soon joined by another couple of bandsmen who had been at practice on Col. Bogey, Home Sweet Home, and God Save, the three hit tunes of the time . . . Martin Dunne, Postmaster, was down like a flash from upstairs demanding 'What the hell [is this] row?'. The Senior Constable, seldom seen out after dark, 'ahem-ed' his way around the corner and demanded to know what was all the shouting, bellowing and screeching about—were they mad or going mad.

If there was any anxiety over how an adolescent country might measure up against its senior British relative whose military exploits were vast, Gallipoli removed all doubts. A legend was born, one which for many Australians remains an affirmation of national worth today. As the Anzacs are remembered at the break of dawn on an autumn morning each year, a nation is reminded: they had been tested, and not found wanting.

AIRBORNE

It was unnatural and dangerous, an occupation for daring young men. In the early 20th century, flying just wasn't natural. But on 16 July 1914, a charming, reckless Frenchman 'soared gracefully into the air like a carrier pigeon' according to newspaper reports at the time, and set course from Melbourne to Sydney. And in doing so a new word entered the Australian lexicon: airmail.

Maurice Guillaux, the son of a French cartwright, was one of those daring young men. Legend has it he was the founder of what the more discreet might refer to as the mile-high club, although looking at his moth-like Bleriot monoplane —now suspended from the ceiling in Sydney's Powerhouse Museum—to achieve such a feat would appear impossible. The 31-year-old pioneered Australia's skies and paved the way for the greatest Australian flying ace of them all, Smithy.

Guillaux's entry into history books was by accident, however. As he was pulling the crowds across the countryside with his daredevil acrobatics, another daring young man was preparing for Australia's first aerial mail delivery between the country's two largest cities. Contracted for the flight was an American known as 'Wizard'—Arthur Burr Stone—who had carried out the first flight in Brisbane two years earlier, landing his monoplane on the Exhibition Grounds.

Anticipating keen public interest, the PMG's Department issued souvenir postcards leading up to the event, featuring Wizard with his Metz-Bleriot. At 1 shilling each plus a penny for postage, these postcards were expected to make up the bulk of the mailbags the aviator was to carry on his historic flight. That the fine print on the back warned the purchaser that the Postmaster-General would accept 'no responsibility for non-delivery through accident or any cause' only seemed to make it all the more thrilling.

Six weeks before the scheduled flight, the Postmaster-General's carefully laid plans were thrown into disarray. Stone crashed his plane on 1 June, and although he survived, his flying machine was reduced to a pile of matchsticks. It looked unlikely he would be able to rustle up a new aircraft before the appointed day of the flight.

Always looking for the next record, Guillaux needed little persuasion to step in. A month earlier, he had become the first pilot to perform a 'loop the loop' in Australia. The Sydney Morning Herald reported the event:

Two thousand feet [610 metres] in the air something streaked across the heavens like a huge dragon fly. It swung round and round, poised for a minute, and then suddenly dropped perpendicularly towards earth, like a meteor. But before reaching the ground it resumed the horizontal, and skimmed over the heads of the crowd so close that many screamed and others threw themselves to the ground.

New postcards were hastily printed, featuring a suave-looking Guillaux seated in the cockpit of his Bleriot. In early 2008, one such postcard, dated 16 June 1914, and signed by the pilot with greetings in French to the mayor of Ballarat, fetched $30,000 when it went under the hammer at Melbourne's Leski Auctions.

On the morning of 16 July, the Frenchman donned his fur-lined jacket and signature tri-coloured silk scarf, and made his way to Melbourne's Showgrounds. As the tiny plane's 60-horsepower engine spluttered into action at 9.15 a.m., the Deputy Postmaster-General handed Guillaux a 40-pound (18-kilo) mailbag containing 2500 postcards and letters, and Australia's first domestic air freight—Lipton tea and OT lemon squash cordial. You would have thought he'd at least been given a decent bottle of Beaujolais, says aviation journalist Jeff Watson. 'It was an astonishing feat for its day. The weather was truly appalling. Guillaux landed no less than seven times, spent about nine and a half hours in the air carrying 1785 postcards at a bob a time.' That's about 20 cents in today's money.

The epic 930-kilometre journey was threatened by strong winds and pelting rain. Despite the bleak weather, excited crowds gathered at each of Guillaux's seven pit stops, where 4-gallon tins of Shell fuel were at the ready. With no aerial map to guide him, the aviator followed the railway line. Below him trains tooted, people waved and cheered and church bells rang out. At Seymour, Wangaratta, Albury, Wagga Wagga, Harden and Goulburn, bonfires were lit in open fields to guide Guillaux to his landing points. The whole operation almost went to plan. On the final stretch from Goulburn, however, Guillaux realised he was running out of fuel. He was forced to make an emergency landing in Liverpool, now a suburb in south-western Sydney.

On 18 July, Guillaux was finally in sight of the Sydney skyline. He performed half a dozen victory laps above the city, waving to the cheering crowds, before landing in Moore Park. The Governor-General, Sir Ronald Munro Ferguson, was the first among a crowd of several hundred to congratulate him, before he was lifted shoulder high and the band struck up 'La Marseillaise'. Not only had the Frenchman successfully completed Australia's first aerial mail delivery, he had also set a world distance record for the carriage of mail by air. It had taken him two and a half days and a total of nine and a half hours' flying time. In that time, the mail train could have travelled from Melbourne to Sydney and back again, but that wasn't the point.

Two weeks later, fighting broke out in Europe. Britain was at war and therefore Australia. One of the casualties was to be Guillaux himself, who served as a test pilot with the French air force and an instructor with the Australian Flying Corps in England.

It is not hard to imagine just how vulnerable those early air pioneers must have felt, despite their outward bravado. A bit of wire and glue was all that seemed to hold these early aircraft together. And of course there were no air traffic controllers or radar. A year before Guillaux's historic Melbourne to Sydney flight, the aviator described in an interview his fear after realising he was lost over a stretch of ocean:

After half an hour, I descended a little to look for land. To my surprise, and quite frankly admitting my great alarm, I saw only water. The situation was not a happy one. It was nightfall and I was over the open sea. I did not know where I was . . . the wind continued to drive against me, and the mist obscured the horizon. Thus I flew for more than an hour and a half without seeing land again. The time seemed long, very long. Of course, I had confidence; but this long day, this interminable journey from 4 o'clock in the morning, this continual tension, plus the sea-sickness that I had suffered—all this combined to plunge me into a profound melancholy. It was in truth the anguish of the child who is afraid of the night.

Finally, a little before 7 o'clock, very low on the horizon I caught sight of the flat coastline. And no landscape—even the most beautiful in the world—has ever given me such delight as the countryside which now greeted my eyes after such a long absence.

❊

'The plane was great in War but it will be greater in Peace,' predicted Captain Harry Butler after returning from the

Great War. 'This is the beginning of a new era in mail and passenger transport.'

And so it was. In his Bristol monoplane, Butler went on to carry the mail from Adelaide to his hometown of Minlaton, 197 kilometres away on the Yorke Peninsula. There were other young Australian war-hero aviators looking for a challenge as well. And four of them were about to risk their lives in a bid to bring the mail all the way from Britain. The incentive was a small fortune offered by the Commonwealth—£10,000 prize money for the first Australian-manned flight from England to Australia completed within 30 days. The sum, offered in 1919, would be the equivalent today of about $600,000.

With far greater career opportunities awaiting Australian ex-service pilots in Europe, Prime Minister Billy Hughes had been searching for an attention-grabbing stunt to lure the pilots home for some time. His government and the opposition had a less optimistic view of his plan, however, and refused to grant the funds needed to subsidise the competing crews. So the idea of a race was born, and with the prize of £10,000 the challenge was issued by the government on 19 March, 'with a view to stimulating aerial activity', according to the Treasurer, William Watt.

Among the ex-World War I flying aces who immediately began spruiking for sponsorship to compete was Ross Macpherson Smith, an Australian who had flown with Lawrence of Arabia and was twice awarded the Military Cross during the war. Smith wrote to the British aircraft manufacturers Vickers:

We are thinking of entering the Vimy for the Australian flight and consider that the best way would be to exchange the wheels for floats on the way, say in Italy and take an oversea route landing in various sea ports on the way. Do you think this exchange would be possible, and if so how do you consider that it would affect the performance of the machine, weight carrying capacity, etc. It would be necessary to carry fuel for single flights of 1,000 miles [1600 kilometres].

When war broke out, Adelaide-born Smith, the son of Scottish immigrants, had signed up as a Sergeant in the 3rd Light Horse Regiment. He fought in Gallipoli and in the Battle of Romani in the Sinai before joining the Australian Flying Corps in 1917. According to the Australian War Memorial, as a pilot with the No. 1 Squadron Smith took part in attacks, aerial photography missions, and bombing raids on Turkish forces. On one occasion he landed 'in the face of the enemy to rescue a downed comrade'.

Vickers, an engineering firm which had started out in Sheffield casting iron church bells almost a century earlier, had made its fortune manufacturing armaments during the war. Smith was a war hero and Vickers, realising the potential publicity such an event could generate, handed over a brand-new Vimy bomber. Says the renowned historic aircraft aviator Lang Kidby, it was the equivalent of a modern-day pilot being given a space shuttle. The aircraft certainly had a promising pedigree: it was the sister ship to the one Alcock and Brown had been given for their historic transatlantic crossing some months earlier.

Smith put together his four-man crew. His brother Keith Macpherson Smith would serve as co-pilot and navigator, while Sergeant Jim Bennett and Sergeant Wally Shiers, with whom Smith had flown from Egypt to India the previous year, were the mechanics.

The Smith team was not without rivals. Nine crews submitted entries, although four would later withdraw. Another two ex-servicemen were busy planning their return to England to compete in the race. Paul 'Ginty' McGinness and Hudson Fysh had already secured sponsorship from the wealthy Yanko pastoralist Sir Samuel McCaughey, who had donated the plane McGinness flew throughout the war. The duo's former flight-sergeant engineer, Arthur Baird, had agreed to join them. But on 25 July, Sir Samuel dropped dead of a heart attack. The executors of his will refused to hand over the money, and McGinness and Fysh were obliged to pull out.

Meanwhile, Smith and his crew got ready to fly into history. They had secured sponsorship from Shell, which had agreed to provide fuel for the plane at pit stops in France, Italy, Egypt, Syria, Iraq, Persia, India, Burma, Singapore, the Dutch East Indies and Timor. The longest stretch of the flight was 1600 kilometres and their Vimy had a proven record of 2800 kilometres non-stop.

On 12 November 1919, the four Australians took off from Hounslow, England. The weather conditions were appalling and on take-off the plane almost bowled over a photographer who had ignored warnings to stay off the tarmac. In their Vimy biplane with Rolls Royce Eagle engines, the Smiths would have been lucky to get 150 kilometres an hour, says Jeff Watson, and with an 'open cockpit, bloody cold'. On board the flimsy aircraft was one bag of mail, including a letter written by Smith two days earlier, addressed to Miss Violet Fraser:

Dear Violet, This is just a wee letter about nothing at all which I am going to try and fly to Australia and then send back to you. We leave very shortly in a Vickers Vimy machine and I have great hopes of getting there.

The Vimy's registration was G-EAOU, and the crew were only half-joking when they said it stood for 'God 'elp all of us'. The flight was plagued by mishaps. Either enraged or simply terrified, a bull attempted to charge the plane as it prepared to take off at Allahabad in India. Then a hawk flew into the plane's port propeller over Calcutta. Smith pressed on regardless—after all, the crew had already overcome a far greater life-threatening challenge. After landing in Crete, Bennett and Shiers had noticed a huge crack in the induction pipes. They had no spare parts and couldn't even lay their hands on a welder. What they did have, however, was a box of chewing gum. Smith and his crew started to chew. When the box was empty, they stuck the results of their efforts on the exhaust manifold and started up the engines. The heat from the exhaust made the chewing gum set as hard as rock. And that gum stayed put all the way to Darwin.

Meanwhile, one of Guillaux's countrymen was threatening to steal the Smith team's thunder. Almost a month before Smith and his crew took off in the race, Etienne Poulet had set out to become the first to fly to Australia from Paris. On the day the Smith Vimy left Hounslow for Australia, Poulet was already halfway there. But engine trouble over Burma forced him to abandon his record-setting attempt.

On 10 December, Smith approached Australia's coastline. He had spotted HMAS *Sydney* and arranged for the ship to help guide his aircraft towards Darwin. Before landing to a wild reception, he wrote a letter to the ship's captain thanking him, placed the message in a bottle and dropped it into the sea. The four men landed on Australian soil as national heroes; the Smith brothers would each later receive a knighthood for exceptional services to aviation. At an average speed of 137 kilometres per hour, the Vimy had spent a total of 135 hours in the air. The flight had taken 28 days. If the mailbags Smith had taken on board in England had gone by their usual route, the ship would have arrived just a few days later.

Darwin's postmaster, E.J. Cook, 'posted' Australia's first official piece of transcontinental airmail two days later. He handed Smith a letter, and the crew prepared for the first north-to-south air crossing of the nation.

'The occasion is unprecedented in the history of the Commonwealth,' Cook wrote. 'Its importance cannot be over-estimated . . . as doubtless the aeroplane will bridge the vast, sparsely inhabited interior, and provide the means whereby the transmission of mails will be greatly facilitated.'

The route to Melbourne had been well prepared for them by none other than their erstwhile competitors, Ginty McGinness and Hudson Fysh. After their disappointing withdrawal, they had accepted an assignment from the Department of Defence to survey the air race route from Longreach in Queensland to Darwin, via the Roper River and Katherine. Fysh had been one of the first to congratulate Smith upon his arrival in Darwin, having prepared the landing ground himself.

Almost four months earlier, he and McGinness had set out in a Model-T Ford for a 2179-kilometre journey through the outback, much of which had never been crossed by a motor vehicle before. The gruelling 51-day trip, laying supplies for the competitors at various points along the way, would prompt Fysh to later write: 'We were convinced of the important part aircraft would eventually play in transporting mail, passengers and freight over the sparsely populated and practically roadless areas of western and northern Queensland and North Australia.'

Exactly a year and a day after McGinness and Fysh left Longreach in their Model-T Ford to prepare the air race route, the pair, along with former flight sergeant Baird, would purchase the first aircraft for their newly established company, the Western Queensland Auto Aero Service Limited. It would quickly go on to become the Queensland and Northern Territory Aerial Services Limited, and almost as quickly become known by its famous acronym, Qantas.

Smith may have taken just 28 days to get the mail from England to Australia, but it was to take him another 76 days to get it down to Melbourne. Serious engine trouble in Charleville delayed the flight for seven weeks. Collecting more mail along the way, including in Sydney, Smith finally handed some 364 letters over to the Prime Minister's Department on 25 February 1920. Under the instructions of Prime Minister Hughes, a commemorative label and date stamp had been prepared.

Designed by Gallipoli war veteran and artist Lieutenant George Courtney Benson, it was to become known among philatelists as the Ross Smith air stamp, with envelopes bearing its insignia fetching up to $15,000 today. Smith had, in fact, been hoping for a postage stamp to commemorate the first England to Australia flight. But that wasn't to happen for another 50 years.

In August 1920, another two Australians touched down in Darwin. Ray Parer and J.C. McIntosh may have left London in their Airco DH-9 well after the Smith team had claimed the £10,000 prize, but they were nevertheless pronounced the only other successful entrants in Billy Hughes's race. With them they brought Australia's first piece of international air cargo—a bottle of Peter Dawson whisky for Hughes himself.

In 1994, Lang Kidby, who had served 14 years as an army pilot with the Aviation Corps, set out to re-enact Smith's historic flight in a Vickers Vimy replica he had built himself. He has a lot of respect for the old World War I bomber.

> We look at the old aeroplanes and we see how they're made of fabric and wire and wood and you say 'My God, I'd never fly these aeroplanes today'. But we've got to consider it from the time. Ross Smith was given a Vickers Vimy, which was the latest development, the best that science and industry could offer.

Cutting-edge aviation technology could not protect the life of Ross Macpherson Smith, however. On 13 April 1922, the Vickers Viking amphibian he was testing at Weybridge near London spun out of control and plunged 305 metres to the ground. Smith was killed instantly, along with his long-serving mechanic Jim Bennett. Keith Smith witnessed the crash, which was caused, an investigation later found, by pilot error.

Smith had yet to turn 30. The men's bodies were transported

to Australia and Smith was given a state funeral in his hometown of Adelaide.

✻

Sea mail wasn't getting any faster. The month-long journey of the Royal Mails hadn't changed in decades, nor would it improve over the course of the 20th century. The standing record for the mail run between England and Australia remains 27 days, set by P&O–Orient's RMS *Oriana* on her maiden voyage in December 1961.

Airmail was clearly the way of the future, and in a country as vast as Australia, innovations in aviation were as essential for transcontinental communication as they were internationally. As the pioneers of the Australian skies clocked up countless 'firsts' and further national and world records, their triumphant landings would inevitably culminate in the thud of a mailbag dropping on the landing strip. While pilots were anxious to keep their loads light, even in air races such as the MacRobertson race from London to Melbourne in 1934, space could always be found for a mailbag or two.

Overnight rail transport still remained the most efficient way of conveying the mails between the cities. But in remote areas not serviced by rail, air transport developed faster as a matter of necessity.

In early 1920, McGinness and Fysh were once more looking for financial backers, but this time more was at stake than just a race. If a regular air service was needed anywhere, it was in Queensland, where outback roads still ranged from poor to non-existent and flooding rivers could cut off already isolated communities from the rest of the world for months.

A fortuitous encounter between McGinness and a wealthy grazier would lay the foundations for what was to become Qantas.

The pilot came across Fergus McMaster stranded in the sandy bed of the Cloncurry River. His car had broken an axle and McGinness gave him a hand. The two got talking and McMaster was fascinated by the ex-serviceman's tales of his adventures in aviation. Joined by Fysh back in Brisbane, the three men began outlining plans to create what promised to be the country's first airline. McMaster then set about collecting investors from among his wealthy acquaintances, while McGinness and Fysh, along with Arthur Baird, headed to Sydney. At Mascot Aerodrome two Avro aircraft were ordered, in the name of the Western Queensland Auto Aero Service Limited. The company officially came into being at Brisbane's Gresham Hotel three months later, on 16 November. The plan was to initially offer joy rides and short passenger trips from the company's Winton base (which later moved to Longreach), then move into mail delivery. Now chairman of the new company, McMaster approached Billy Hughes with the idea of establishing an airmail route from Charleville to Cloncurry. Hughes reportedly told him to come back in 10 years.

By the middle of the following year, however, the Federal Government clearly had had a change of heart. But it was to Western Australia, not Queensland, that the Department of Defence looked to establish the country's first scheduled airmail service. In May 1921, the government called for tenders to operate a weekly airmail and passenger service between Geraldton and Derby. The initial contract would be limited to 12 months, with a government subsidy not exceeding £25,000. The government's Civil Aviation Branch would take responsibility for constructing the landing strips.

It was a huge run, stretching more than 1900 kilometres, with scheduled stops at Carnarvon, Onslow, Roebourne, Port Hedland and Broome. According to Fred Niven, who worked with Ansett for 37 years and served as the company's unofficial historian, the route flew over some of the most isolated and sparsely populated areas of the country. While the entire population of Western Australia was about 335,000 in 1921, the expanse between Geraldton and Derby was home to more than five million sheep. Travel between stations was still being made by horse, donkey or camel, because there were few roads to speak of.

With just two months in which to tender, a former Royal Flying Corps pilot by the name of Norman Brearley cabled the Bristol Aeroplane Company in England. With a respectable cruising speed of 136 kilometres an hour, the company's three-seater, 250-horsepower Puma-engined Bristol 28 Tourer Coupé biplanes looked ideal. Might he have six, please? Bristol replied in the affirmative, promising Brearley that if his tender was successful, the aircraft could be delivered by ship to Australia by early November at the latest. On 2 August 1921, the government advised Brearley he had won the tender. The contract demanded that Australia's first weekly airmail service commence operation on 5 December. He had just four months to prepare.

Brearley had trained as a mechanic in Western Australia before travelling to England in 1915 to join the Royal Flying Corps. The following year he was badly wounded over France.

He was sent home to Perth to recover, but his love of flying ensured he didn't stay there long. By the war's end, he had become commander of a flying instructors' school in England. He returned to Australia the following year, bringing with him two Avro 504Js, a few spare parts and a wealth of aviation experience and expertise.

Gathering on the shores of the Swan River, crowds gaped in awe at Brearley's daring aerobatics. His first public flying demonstration, on 2 August 1919 at the Western Australia Cricket Association Oval, was accompanied by a band. His reputation grew, and the wealthy members of Perth society were soon happily forking out £5—more than the average weekly wage—on 10-minute joy flights with the ex-serviceman. Soon he was providing charter flights throughout the state's entire south-west.

The government contract to deliver the mail gave birth to Western Australian Airways. Brearley launched his company's first prospectus on 29 August 1921, with nominal capital of £50,000. By then, he had already signed the deal with the Bristol Aeroplane Company. The terms were strictly cash on delivery—£14,000 for the six Bristol Tourers, including spare parts. They were to arrive just 10 days before the service was scheduled to start. In addition to the mail, the Tourers' cargo holds were large enough to carry essential equipment such as spare parts, tools and food, but not much else. If drinking water was required in an emergency, the planes' radiators would have to do. Six planes required six pilots and Western Australian Airways' first employees were Len Taplin, Bob Fawcett, Arthur Blake, Val Abbott and an aviator the world was about to hear a lot more of, Charles Kingsford 'Smithy' Smith.

The first signs that Australia's inaugural airmail service might be heading for disaster were evident when Brearley conducted a survey of the landing grounds built by the Civil Aviation Branch. According to Fred Niven, the government had not been prepared to spend large amounts on the construction and had contracted most work out to local authorities. And some of the results would have been downright laughable, if they hadn't been so dangerous. Clearly at least one landing site had been built by someone who had never seen an aeroplane before, Niven says. It had been constructed 'as a flattened circle, just 31 metres in diameter and surrounded by 60-centimetre-high white stones, to, in theory, make it easier for the pilot to spot!' Brearley complained to the government that the standard of the landing sites—including the main base in Geraldton—was unacceptable. He was ignored.

On the Monday morning of 5 December 1921, three Western Australian Airlines Tourers left Geraldton with the first bags of mail. Len Taplin led the squadron in one plane, followed 100 metres behind by Bob Fawcett and a company mechanic, Edward Broad, in another. Brearley brought up the rear, bringing with him two passengers—the pastoralist Michael Patrick Durack and a gentleman by the name of Geoff Jacoby—to mark the historic occasion.

Less than an hour out of Geraldton, Taplin began having trouble with his engine. He decided to make an emergency landing on the Murchison House Station. Seeing Taplin descend, Fawcett reduced height and went to circle, to see if Taplin needed assistance. It was a fatal mistake. The slowing of his engine caused it to stall and the plane plummeted to the ground. Fawcett and Broad were killed instantly.

Brearley had not witnessed the crash. He had flown over Taplin on the ground and landed about 3 kilometres away, after failing to sight the second plane and fearing something had gone wrong. Eventually, two Aboriginal station hands came galloping towards him on horseback, and informed him of the disaster. Fawcett and Broad were buried near where they had fallen, in the station's cemetery the same day. Australia's first airmail delivery had ended in tragedy.

The devastated pilots flew their Tourers back to Perth the following day, with Brearley vowing his remaining men would stay grounded until the Civil Aviation Branch fixed its landing sites. The mail was transported overland and taken onwards by steamer to Derby. A subsequent government investigation found that pilot error had caused the crash, concluding the 'pilot banked too steeply in landing in rough country'.

Government expenditure on the route had been woefully inadequate, says Niven. Just £200 and £190 had been spent constructing the main landing sites at Geraldton and Derby respectively. The Geraldton site eventually had to be abandoned altogether, as was the site at Port Hedland, which had cost £300 to build. Just £35 had been spent at the Wallal stop between Port Hedland and Broome, and a ridiculous £18.15s at Roebourne. In many of these areas, the mail went back to delivery by horseback, and it would be another three months before Brearley agreed, on 3 March 1922, to recommence services.

Australia's pioneering airmail cost money as well as lives. Western Australian Airlines' fee for delivery by airmail started at an additional threepence for a standard letter. For parcels, steep incremental charges were determined according to weight. For passengers, the two-and-a-half-day flight was calculated at a shilling per mile. It would cost the equivalent of three months' average earnings for a £60 seat on the Geraldton to Derby flight.

Two years to the day after the tragedy at Murchison House Station, Brearley's airmail contract was renewed for a further three years. The government had added a provision for extending the route southwards, from Geraldton to Perth, allowing the company to compete directly with the railways. And on 26 May 1929, Australia's first regular interstate airmail delivery took place, with Western Australian Airlines carrying the mailbags from Brearley's hometown of Perth to the late Ross Macpherson Smith's hometown of Adelaide.

※

When outback pioneer Alexander Kennedy made his first journey between Charleville and Cloncurry in the early 1870s, the 930-kilometre trek by bullock wagon had taken eight months. So it was with great reverence that the octogenarian was helped on board Qantas's maiden airmail flight, along with 108 letters, on 2 November 1922. The fact he was also one of Frank McMaster's recruited investors—and a member of the company's provisional board—undoubtedly helped secure his No. 1 passenger ticket. This time the Charleville to Cloncurry trip was to take two days. As Kennedy reportedly said as he climbed into the cockpit behind Hudson Fysh: 'Be damned to the doubters.'

Not all went to plan, as Fysh recalled in his book, *Qantas Rising*.

The Armstrong Whitworth was wheeled out of the hangar at the first streak of dawn, many willing hands helping to push her to the then uneven surface of the stony 'tarmac'. The 160hp Beardmore engine sprang to life after Baird and his helpers had given the propeller a few turns, and flickering flames jetted from the exhaust stubs. I climbed into the cockpit and ran the engine up. Yes, she gave her full revs and all was in readiness. Kennedy climbed in, brushing off assistance as he groped for the foot-niches in the side of the fuselage, and then he was settled with safety belt adjusted. Baird was aboard too. The chocks were pulled away from the wheels, and out we taxied to the far corner of the aerodrome.

The wind was light and fitful, coming from the north-east in warm puffs. It was going to be a scorching western day. When I opened up the throttle with a roar we gathered motion, careening towards the far fence, but we did not seem to be getting the usual lift, the revs were down a shade, and the old AW refused to come unstuck. I shut off and taxied back for another try.

Fysh was to abort the take-off a total of three times before returning to the hangar and wheeling out the Avro 504K, an English-made, Australian-assembled aircraft the company had bought 18 months earlier. A nonplussed Kennedy—and the mailbags—were apologetically transferred. The fourth attempt at take-off from Longreach was a success, and the airmail headed for its first stop, Winton, just 35 minutes late.

Two years had passed since a handshake between three men in a Brisbane pub had signalled the birth of an airline. Declining to take Billy Hughes's advice to 'come back in 10 years', McMaster, McGinness, Fysh and Baird instead issued a prospectus offering 15,000 ordinary shares at £1 each. Although the airline's enduring symbol would not appear until 1947, the Flying Kangaroo remains airborne as it heads towards its first centenary.

On the other side of the continent, however, the badge of endurance was not to be for Western Australian Airlines. In 1934, Brearley lost his monopoly of the western skies when the Federal Government decided to extend the Perth to Wyndham route to Daly Waters in the Northern Territory. New tenders were called for and the government awarded the five-year contract to a rival company, MacRobertson Miller Aviation.

Some 15 years after pioneering Australia's first airmail route, Brearley sold his company for £25,000 to Adelaide Airways and prepared for what proved to be a long retirement. He died in 1989, just before his 100th birthday. The company which emerged from the sale, Australian National Airways, was to go on to dominate domestic air travel for more than 20 years. On 3 October 1957, a payment of £3.3 million handed ANA over to Reginald Myles Ansett.

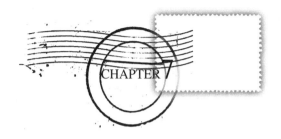

FROM BEHIND ENEMY
LINES

The glamour of air travel in the 1920s was not lost on the Post Office. Nothing could impress the recipient of a letter quite as much as a 'forwarded by airmail' stamp on an envelope, which the PMG's Department began doing in 1926. Airmail still cost twice as much as surface mail, but, with the help of the Post Office's 'for that urgent letter' slogan, prestige and speed made it popular. In remote centres, such as Broken Hill in New South Wales, the airmail would arrive two and a half days earlier than the surface mail.

In 1924, interstate deliveries began with a Sydney to Adelaide route by Australian Aerial Services. The same year, Qantas introduced the four-passenger DH50 to its Charleville–Cloncurry travellers. With its enclosed cockpit, the DH50 ensured that the days of passengers donning helmet and goggles were over. The following year the route was extended north to Camooweal and then further still to Normanton. And when the first service from Charleville to Brisbane was launched in 1929, passengers were mightily impressed with the novel inclusion of a toilet on board the DH61 *Apollo*. Qantas's mail and passenger routes were now stretching 2380 kilometres across Queensland. Meanwhile, another Australian flying ace was becoming an international celebrity, and he would go on to pioneer more long-distance routes than any pilot in history.

Handsome, debonair, charming and reckless, Charles Kingsford Smith, it seemed, had walked straight out of a Mills & Boon novel. Adding to the glamour was the fact that this son of a Brisbane banker had worked as a stunt pilot in Hollywood after the war. Returning home to tackle the dangers and distances of the Australian outback by air, he dreamt of starting his own airline. In a letter sent to his parents during the war, he had written: 'I have discovered one thing about flying and that is that my future for whatever it may be worth, is bound up with it.'

Kingsford Smith fought in Gallipoli before joining the Australian Flying Corps in late 1916. Just five months later he was selected to join Britain's Royal Flying Corps (RFC). In August 1917, as a Second Lieutenant in the No.23 Squadron, he came under attack over France from three German planes. He was wounded and shot down, his plane having sustained damage from some 180 bullet holes. Wounded in the foot, he had to have several toes amputated. The injury earned the 20-year-old 'Smithy' a Military Cross 'for conspicuous gallantry and devotion to duty' but signalled the end of his fighting days.

Promoted to Lieutenant the following year, he played out the final year of the war as an RFC flying instructor.

Danger and adventure acted as magnets to Smithy, so the challenge of the England to Australia air race announced by the Federal Government in 1919 immediately attracted him. It is believed Billy Hughes prevented him from participating, however, on the grounds he lacked navigational experience. So Smithy remained in England and formed a partnership with Cyril Maddocks. The two began conducting joyflights to fund passage to the United States, where Smithy had dreams of making the first transpacific flight. Sponsors proved elusive, however, and he soon found himself earning a living in California's fledgling film industry. The work was thrilling but dangerous. Some accounts of Smithy's life say he returned to Australia after witnessing a colleague plunge to his death during a particularly daring stunt. Other accounts claim he joined an air circus and was compelled to return home only after being swindled by the circus's promoters. Either way, in 1921 he landed back in Australia virtually penniless, before being rescued by Norman Brearley's invitation to join his team of airmail pioneers.

Six years later, Smithy returned to Sydney to form a partnership with another daring aviator. Charles Ulm shared Smithy's vision of flying across the world's largest ocean, but the duo first set their sights on a more attainable venture: securing the government contract to deliver the Adelaide–Perth mail. Their tender failed. There was nothing for Smithy and Ulm to do but to go on and make history.

In June 1927, Smithy, Ulm and their Bristol Tourer set their first record. At 10 days and five hours, their round-Australia journey had more than halved the existing record. This grand feat enabled them to secure sponsorship for the long-planned Pacific crossing from the New South Wales Government and the wealthy Melbourne businessman and philanthropist Sidney Myer. With the assistance of Californian oil magnate G. Allan Hancock, the duo secured a three-engined Fokker plane, which they renamed the *Southern Cross*. Together with two American crewmen, Harry Lyon and Jim Warner, Smithy and Ulm flew into history on 31 May 1928, when they left Oakland, California, and commenced the 11,891-kilometre journey over the Pacific. They landed in Brisbane eight days later, where they were greeted by a cheering crowd of over 25,000 people.

Smithy would go on to set and beat countless records. He flew the *Southern Cross* to England in record time, crossed the Atlantic and completed the first round-the-world flight. Everyone loved the charismatic Smithy for his stamina, guts and swagger. But the Post Office loved him for his incredible ability to rescue the mail. To commemorate Smithy's exploits, the Post Office issued a stamp depicting the *Southern Cross* in March 1931. The aviator had earlier been invited to appraise the design and offer suggestions. He responded accordingly to the PMG's Department's head, Harry Percy Brown:

My dear Mr Brown . . . I congratulate you upon the general outlay of the stamp, but offer you the following small alteration purely as a suggestion. That the machine's direction be reversed (as this was the direction in which she flew around the world). This would enable the 'USU' to be put on the correct wing, as it is at present upon the wrong wing . . .

Smithy always made sure his *Southern Cross* flew the right way. The following month British Imperial Airway's first experimental return airmail flight from Britain to Australia crashed in Timor. Who better to rescue the mail and bring it on to Australia? The DH66 Hercules *City of Cairo* had crash-landed near Koepang. Miraculously, the pilots escaped unharmed, but they, along with the mail, were stranded. Up until then, the two-week flight had gone to plan. The pilots had met the mailbags in Karachi from another Imperial aircraft, the *City of Coventry*, which had departed London on 4 April. The crash was a blow to the first venture in what was eventually to become the Empire Route. But it was a bonanza for the newspapers which, following the announcement that Smithy would bring home the mail in the *Southern Cross*, reported the rescue mission in sensational daily instalments.

On 23 April *The Age* reported Smithy's arrival in Darwin from Sydney with co-pilot Scotty Allan, to pick up clearance papers for Timor. The Shell Company had 'done everything possible to ensure a safe and speedy trip', including laying down supplies of oil and spirit in Koepang. As Smithy touched down in Koepang the following day it was 'Southern Cross to the Rescue' and as he triumphantly returned to Darwin on the third day, the press's camera bulbs flashed wildly as Smithy emerged from the plane with the *City of Cairo*'s grateful pilots and 20 bags of mail. Aircraft were on standby to take the mail on to Brisbane and Sydney. It was an Anzac Day to remember, with the President of the Returned Soldiers' Association pronouncing it fitting that 'an Australian had been able to carry on the job' and the veterans were 'proud to have as a digger the ace of aces'.

The flight which had captured a nation translated into huge sales for the Post Office, with staff working round the clock to keep up with demand. With Smithy on the job, everyone wanted their letter to be on that test flight back to Britain. Mailbags flooded into Darwin from across the country, and according to newspaper reports, the 'philatelists caused the most delay'. When Smithy finally took off from Darwin on 27 April for the first leg of the return flight, there were 32,000 letters stowed in the *Southern Cross*. He flew on to Burma and handed the mail over to British Imperial Airways, for the final leg of the trip to Britain.

It was to be the first of many such missions. A matter of months later, another aircraft going in the opposite direction crashed in Kedah on the Malay Peninsula, and once again it was Smithy who went to the rescue. Smithy flew to London and returned with the Christmas mail.

The events of 1931 had not all been tales of success, however. In the same month the Post Office had released its *Southern Cross* stamp, the airline Smithy and Ulm had founded a year earlier suffered a devastating blow. On 21 March, raging storms over the Snowy Mountains caused a Sydney to Melbourne flight to crash, killing six passengers along with the pilot and co-pilot. The wreckage of the VH-UMF *Southern Cloud* was not to be found for another 27 years. Smithy and Ulm's Australian National Airways (not to be confused with the identically named company which came into being five years later) was further rocked by the crash of the *Southern Sun* later that year, while attempting to take off in Malaysia to carry the mail from Australia to England. The loss, along with the ongoing effects of the Depression, ultimately caused the

Plate 1: Isaac Nichols. This impression of Australia's first postmaster is based on an artist's impression and one of Isaac's living descendants. *Artwork by Iain McKellar*

Inset Plate 2: This stamp, featuring a drawing of Isaac boarding a ship, was issued to commemorate the Australian Post Office's 150th anniversary in 1959. It too was based on another artist's impression; there is no other representation of Isaac. *Australia Post*

Above Plate 3: Isaac Nichols ran Australia's first postal service from a ground-floor room in his substantial home on George Street, pictured here second from the left. *Carmichael, John, 1803–1857, Plate no. 2 of: Select views of Sydney, New South Wales, National Library of Australia*

Below left Plate 4: Australia's very first stamp was issued in 1850 and known as the 'Sydney View'. Hope is seated on a bale of wheat overlooking Sydney Harbour, with allegorical symbols for industry and commerce in the background. *Australia Post*

Below right Plate 5: A postcard from Paris to Jersey, Channel Islands, demonstrating the practice of cross-writing to minimise the number of sheets used, circa 1875. *By permission of Richard Breckon*

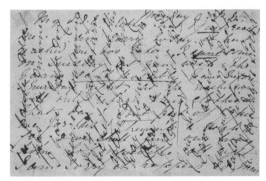

Plate 6: A Cobb & Co. coach packed to the rafters … *Australia Post*

Plate 7: … and bogged to the axles. *Australia Post*

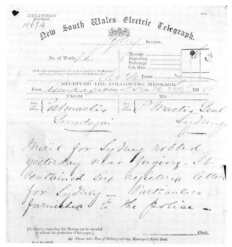

Plate 8: A scrawled telegram from the Postmaster of Gundagai to the Postmaster of Sydney announcing that the mail had been robbed: 'Mail for Sydney robbed yesterday near Jugiong. It contained six registered letters for Sydney. Particulars furnished to the police.' *National Archives of Australia: C4076, HN16*

Plate 9: Bardon Post Office, circa 1890: grocer, produce merchant and post office, all rolled into one. *National Archives of Australia: J2879, QTH314/2*

Plate 10: A Travelling Post Office in the early 1900s. Mail was sorted on long train trips up until the 1980s. *Australia Post*

Plate 11: A stamp cancelling device, first introduced about 1878. *Australia Post*

Plate 12: Melbourne postmen of the 1890s—
then called letter carriers—wearing the
summer uniform. *National Archives of Australia:
C4076, HN28*

Plate 13: Female telephonists at
the first Brisbane central manual
telephone exchange, 1910.
National Archives of Australia:
J2879, QTH321/2

Plate 14: The 'Absurd Kangaroo'. Australia's first Commonwealth stamp of 1913 was quite unconventional: the concept of placing an 'absurd' animal on a national stamp was ludicrous to some; the tufts of grass which sprouted at the marsupial's feet like a pair of rabbit's ears in the original design released to the public were removed to appease critics. Worse still there was no sign of the monarch. *Australia Post*

Plate 15: The winner of a stamp design competition in 1911: Herman Altmann collected the £100 prize money for his ornate portrait of George V, flanked by emu, kangaroo, crown and each of the six states' emblems. *Australia Post*

Plate 16: The first stamps with a Commonwealth design were issued by New South Wales and Queensland in 1903. *Australia Post*

THE STAMP OF THE COMMONWEALTH.

THE P.M.G.: "What do you think of that?"
AUSTRALIA: "Great Scott! The seven years' drought! I didn't think you'd advertise that!"

Plate 17: A 1912 cartoon in Sydney's *Daily Telegraph* did not favour the kangaroo stamp. *State Library of New South Wales*

Plate 18: The lifeline to home. Men of the 26th Battalion read their mail by their dugouts not far from the front line in France, August 1918. *Australian War Memorial Negative Number E02941*

Inauguration of Australia's Aerial Mail

This mail was carried by M. Guillaux from Melbourne (Vic.) to Sydney (N.S.W.) on his Bleriot Monoplane. The distance covered was approximately 580 miles. Aerial mails have previously been inaugurated in England, France, South Africa, U.S.A. and Germany, but the distance covered by M. Guillaux stands as a record.

"SHELL" BENZINE was used in the transport of this, the first Aerial Mail in Australia. It is noteworthy that the first Aerial Mail in Great Britain was also carried on "SHELL."

Plate 19: A suave-looking Guillaux seated in the cockpit of his Bleriot. This souvenir postcard commemorated Australia's first aerial mail delivery in 1914. *By permission of Chris Lloyd*

Plate 20: A publicity poster encouraging the public to use airmail services, circa 1935. *Australia Post*

Plate 21: 'Smithy' handing over the first airmail to Postmaster Hurtle Bald in Darwin. The mail was retrieved from the crashed *City of Cairo* in Timor in 1931. Bald was later killed in the first air raid attack on Darwin in 1942. *Mayse Young Collection, Northern Territory Library*

Plate 22: A man steps across the abyss as the GPO clock face is removed during the tower deconstruction in 1942. After the fall of Singapore, there were fears the 46-metre GPO tower could act as a beacon to hostile aircraft. The tower was removed stone by stone; each block was listed, numbered and placed into storage where it would remain for 20 years. *National Archives of Australia: C4078, N1974A*

Plate 23: Though air travel had transformed mail delivery, less than half a century ago the Birdsville Track mail route was still being serviced by land—the mail delivered by an outback legend named Tom Kruse. This photograph shows *The Back of Beyond* director John Heyer talking with Tom Kruse, who is sitting in the open top Ford Blitz royal mail truck, on the Birdsville Track in 1954. *By permission of the John Heyer Estate, National Film and Sound Archive*

Plates 24–33: Submissions to the 1955 competition to design the millionth migrant commemorative stamp. Some three hundred stamps were entered, but no winner was ever chosen. *Australia Post*

Plate 34: Jean de Sperati, stamp forger extraordinaire. *Australia Post*

Plate 35: Brett Whiteley's 'unadopted' 1982 stamp design for the 50th anniversary of the Sydney Harbour Bridge. *Australia Post*

Plate 36: 1953 propaganda stamps urging Australian farmers to 'Produce Food!', with rudimentary illustrations of wheat, beef and butter to assist. *Australia Post*

airline to fold after just two years of operation. Smithy's dream of a commercial airline, operating passenger, mail and freight services free of government subsidy, had been short-lived.

A knighthood the following year and a trans-Tasman crossing were not enough to persuade the New Zealand Government to award him a contract for passenger and mail services between Auckland and Singapore. To make ends meet, Smithy opened a flying training school in Sydney and began barnstorming.

In 1933, a 17-year-old girl in outback Australia named Nancy Bird came across the good-looking adventurer offering flights for 10 shillings a ride. She had hoped for a lesson, but of the two aeroplanes Kingsford Smith had on offer, one carried six people, and the other had only a single cockpit. He suggested she come down to Mascot in Sydney as he was starting a flying school later that year. Nancy Bird-Walton was to become one of Australia's aviation heroines, but she would have none of the rumours that surrounded the pilot with a rock-star-like following. Now well into her nineties and crowned an Australian Living Treasure by the National Trust of Australia, Bird-Walton insists Kingsford Smith was a perfect gentleman. 'I've heard stories he was a womaniser and he drank a little too much, but I didn't see that at all,' she says.

I can only speak very highly of him. There's no doubt he was the world's most outstanding pilot. You know the Americans gave Lindbergh a million dollars for flying the Atlantic . . . just as a gift. Poor old Smithy never got any genuine help from the Australian Government at all.

127

While Smithy was training Bird-Walton and other aspiring aviators, Ulm worked on one of the aircraft salvaged from the company's collapse. He renamed the plane *Faith in Australia* and in April 1934 flew the first official mail from Australia to New Zealand. Later that year, he carried the first airmail from Australia to New Guinea and back. On 3 December 1934, Ulm left Oakland, California, for Hawaii in the *Stella Australis* and disappeared. The wreckage was never found.

In May the following year, Smithy finally secured his long-awaited contract for a trans-Tasman airmail service. The maiden flight nearly killed him, along with his navigator Bill Taylor. Some 800 kilometres from the Australian shore, one of the aircraft's three engines cut out. A second engine began rapidly burning oil, also threatening to cut out. In a daring act, Taylor climbed out of the cockpit and collected enough oil from the dead engine to feed the spluttering one. Smithy radioed the PMG's Department with the urgent request: could he please dump the mailbags? Harry Percy Brown responded quickly: 'Dump the mail, but get back.'

In early November 1935, Smithy and his co-pilot, Tommy Pethybridge, were heading back to Australia from England in a new Lockheed Altair that Smithy had christened the *Lady Southern Cross*. They left Allahabad, heading for Singapore; the last record of the *Lady Southern Cross*'s flight was logged at Rangoon, at 1.30 a.m. on 7 November. There the trail goes cold. The 38-year-old Smithy never made it to Singapore. A Royal Air Force search party was dispatched but nothing was found. Almost two years later, a couple of Burmese fishermen found a starboard undercarriage leg on the shore of their island south-east of Rangoon. It is believed the *Lady Southern Cross*, flying in the black of night, hit a rocky peak then plunged into the sea. No remains were ever recovered.

'Kingsford Smith by any definition has to be considered the world's greatest long-distance flyer,' says aviation journalist Jeff Watson. 'He was a brilliant engineer, he was a superb navigator, he was a great pilot. He understood how aeroplanes worked and what a great tragedy it is that this brilliant man is still somewhere up there in the water . . . that he just disappeared . . .'

❋

Like the conquests of Phar Lap, the hullabaloo of an English cricket tour and the scandalous romance between a king and his divorcee lover, the heroic exploits of Charles Kingsford Smith came as welcome diversions during the hard times of the Great Depression. Reactionary government measures of retrenchment and conservative fiscal policy ensnared the economy in an ever-tightening downward spiral. By 1932, around 30 per cent of the workforce—some 337,000 Australians—was jobless. Among a generation still bearing the scars of the Great War, pessimism was endemic and even the national birth rate dropped.

Postal services were not immune to the economic malaise, the PMG's Department calling a halt to development and placing a freeze on employment. But as government policy shifted towards employment creation to kick-start the economy from the mid-1930s, the Post Office moved too, and in the 1930s hundreds of new building and refurbishment projects were completed as part of the nation's recovery plan.

Meanwhile, progress in aviation powered ahead. On 10 December 1934, the Duke of Gloucester cut the red ribbon on Qantas's new DH61 *Diana* and DH50 *Hippomenes*, marking the beginning of what would eventually become part of the Empire Air Mail scheme. A joint venture between Qantas and Britain's Imperial Airways gave birth to Qantas Imperial Airways, with a view to establishing the first regular Australia–England airmail service. Captains Lester Brain and Russell Tapp carried almost 56,000 letters on the inaugural flight that left after the ceremony from Brisbane to Darwin, where the mail was transferred to two Imperial Airways aircraft bound for England via Singapore. The transfer was to have taken place in Singapore, but mechanical problems caused a last-minute change of plans.

The Empire Route—which would come to be known as the Kangaroo Route—was immensely popular. 'Thanks to this new service the London mails for Sydney will reach their destination in 13 days instead of 32 as is the case when they are carried by sea', the international *Union Postale Journal* reported in 1935. Only a war could stop the mail now. On 1 September 1939, Adolf Hitler's incursions into Eastern Europe culminated in the invasion of Poland. Two days later, Australia joined the United Kingdom, France and New Zealand in declaring war on Germany.

Surprisingly, the hostilities did not see the cancellation of Australia's overseas airmail services until the fall of Singapore more than two years later, on 15 February 1942. Domestic postal services continued throughout the war, and the Post Office was busier than ever processing record volumes of mail. With the central role it played in communications, the

PMG's Department was integral to every aspect of the war effort, from laying submarine cables to training servicemen in the use of switchboards and telephone channels. From the department's research laboratories came the first domestic-made coastwatching radar sets. With this development, radar production in Australia began in earnest and in 1942 the Department of Munitions assumed control of the technology.

Billboards placed outside the country's GPOs urged Australians to buy War Savings Certificates and Red Cross Seals. New postmarks warned a nation of the dangers of loose lips, with slogans like 'don't write about ships' and 'don't discuss troop movements'. These were phased out in early 1942, as it was believed such language could upset the enemy, who might hold up the mail's delivery to Australian prisoners of war. All incoming and outgoing mail was subject to censorship, and duly stamped 'opened by censor' at the Post Office.

The mail just kept piling in, with large post offices forced to establish dedicated overseas forces departments. Those in the forces were charged half price for standard postal services, while Australian troops serving overseas were given free postage on surface mail. More than 8000 postal employees had been released for war service, so it was left to those at home to keep the mail moving. In the military camps, full postal and telegraph facilities were invariably serviced by former postal employee servicemen. Out of necessity, an ingenious new device emerged to cope with the sheer volume of mail. Long before the days of e-mail there was V-mail, or, as it was called in Australia, the Airgraph. Originally based on the British 'Airgraph', V-mail was an unusual system for delivering mail from the United States troops to home addresses during World War II. It worked by photographing large amounts of censored mail onto reels of film, which weighed much less than the original would have. The film reels were shipped to the United States, printed out on lightweight photo paper and delivered to the addressee. This saved considerable weight and bulk in a time in which both were hard to manage in a theatre of war. It also eliminated the threat of spies using microdots or invisible ink to send reports. Any microdot would not be photographed with a high enough resolution to be read. The Airgraph service commenced in December 1942 with each member of the Australian forces in the United Kingdom and Middle East permitted to send one Airgraph home for Christmas.

As it was during World War I, communication between the front and home became vital for maintaining the troops' morale. Private Charlie Keys of the 2/15th Battalion wrote from Tobruk: 'What everyone over here waits for is the mail. You have no idea how everyone looks forward to letters from home and everyone keeps them and reads them over and over again.'

The troops not only read their own mail, they read their mates' mail as well. In campaigns like Tobruk and Kokoda, the tropical climate meant paper became easily damp and disintegrated, so there was virtually no reading matter. 'They were desperate for anything to read so it would be natural to pass around what they had to each other,' says World War II historian Mark Johnston.

There was often a shortage of writing material . . . They'd re-use envelopes. If they found a piece of paper, a piece of brown paper for example, or a cigarette packet or a biscuit wrapper. They'd often use that for letters and sometimes without envelopes they'd simply send it in the hope that it would arrive. By and large they did arrive . . . even if they were in envelopes made of bark, or a chocolate wrapper . . . or something of that kind.

Letters would be read and re-read until they fell apart. Private Roy Zuckur, of the 2/24th Battalion, also in Tobruk, wrote:

Hope we soon get out of this hole and get an eyeful of green grass and trees and something cool to drink and a cool or better still a hot bath . . . Write as many letters as you can, we know our letters off by heart we read them so much.

Lasting more than seven months, Tobruk would go down as the longest siege in British imperial military history. Of the 14,000 Australians stationed there, 3009 were killed or wounded between 10 April and 27 November 1941, and a further 941 taken prisoner by the Gemans under Field Marshal Erwin Rommel.

Little more than two months after the siege's end, the front line abruptly arrived on Australia's home soil. On 19 February 1942, a blanket of bombs from 242 Japanese aircraft hailed down on Darwin, killing more than 240 people. Postal worker Murray Fletcher was there and later recounted his story to Joanna Penglase and David Horner for their book *When the War Came to Australia*. He recalled: 'The fellas were working away in the post office and suddenly we became aware of air-raid siren noises and other explosions . . . there was a direct hit on a trench or shelter in the postmaster's residence.'

Based on Douglas Lockwood's 1972 book *Australia's Pearl Harbour, Darwin, 1942, The Age* wrote a detailed account of the attack in 1982, recreating vividly the two raids which took less than an hour to all but flatten the town and sink eight ships. The bodies of seamen would continue to be washed up on the foreshore for weeks afterwards. Looting took place and hundreds of residents fled the town in panic, many heading to the next closest township of Adelaide River, 90 kilometres away.

In desperation, martial law was declared by the Northern Territory's Administrator, Charles Abbott, whose residence and office were destroyed in the raids. Police supervising the evacuation of women, the aged and the wounded were ordered to shoot at the feet of men trying to board the only freight train out of Darwin.

Darwin had been as unprepared as Pearl Harbor had 74 days earlier. Ten American Kittyhawk fighter planes had just flown in, having returned from an attack on Japanese aircraft and submarines, and the harbour was teeming with Allied ships carrying Australian and American troops and supplies. When 188 Zero fighters appeared on the horizon just before 10 a.m., the residents of Darwin assumed they were just more Americans.

'Come and have a look at all the Yanks coming in,' Bruce Acland, a Department of Civil Aviation employee based at Darwin's aerodrome at Parap, reportedly said. 'Who said we haven't got any planes?'

The air-raid siren and the bombing started simultan-
eously, in an attack which observers later described as
curiously 'methodic and unhurried', with the fighter pilots
bringing their planes in so low to the ground their faces could
be seen; even an occasional wave from the attackers was
observed.

In little more than 10 minutes, plumes of smoke were
billowing from 22 listing vessels. The whole town shook as
the 5443-tonne *Neptuna* took a direct hit, instantly killing
45 seamen on board as its cargo of explosives sent a 90-metre
mushroom cloud into the air and spewed white-hot metal into
the water. More than half the people killed during the attack
were aboard those ships. Some 80 died on the ammunition-
laden United States destroyer *Peary* alone. From the nearby
RAN ship *Platypus*, Lieutenant Owen Griffiths watched the
Peary go: 'The ship disintegrated in a burst of flame—she
finally pointed her nose to the sky and disappeared in a
pall of black oily smoke, the gun on her forecastle firing to
the bitter end.' Despite a clearly visible red cross, two bombs
were dropped on the hospital ship *Manunda*, killing 12 people
and injuring 58. Doctors moved to treat the wounded as fires
blazed around them. The *Manunda*'s chief officer, Captain
T. Minto, said they 'worked all the hours God sent treating
the terrible wounds and burns with never a moment to
themselves—manning boats, carrying stretchers, fighting fires
and hoisting the wounded on board'.

The hospital on land also came under fire, but miraculously
only one patient was killed, by a machine-gun bullet. Staff
had ordered patients to lie under their beds, no doubt saving
countless lives. The wounded poured into the shelled Darwin

Hospital, with volunteers holding torches as doctors continued to work through the night.

Elsewhere on land, a team of wharfies were killed when a bomb hit the shed in which they were having their morning smoko. Dozens of men on the wharves were blown into the water, which was awash with burning oil, and at least 22 men were killed there that day. According to *The Age*, a Chinese wharfie called Jimmy Yuen claimed rescuers nearly threw him back into the water, accusing him of being a 'bloody Jap'. His skin was saved by hollering in pure 'Strine', 'Fair go, mates! I'm a bloody wharfie'.

Another bomb blew a train and six trucks into the water. Nine of the Kittyhawk fighter planes were destroyed immediately, and at least four of the pilots were killed. *The Age* recounted the miraculous escape of one Kittyhawk pilot, Lieutenant John Glover:

> As he circled the descending parachute of his comrade Lieutenant Burt Rice to protect him from the Zeros, his plane went into a dive, levelled off as it reached the aerodrome, cart-wheeled several times and smashed into pieces. He walked away from the wreckage, sat down and buried his face in his hands, then was dragged to safety.

Darwin's administrative block, including the police barracks, Government House and the GPO, were reduced to rubble by six 1000-pound (450-kilo) bombs. The bomb shelter under Government House, where the Administrator, his wife and their employees sought refuge, partially caved in when a slab of concrete fell into the shelter, killing Daisy Martin, one of the Abbotts' maids. It was later discovered that the steel door of the strongroom had swung open and jammed in the blast, saving the shelter's occupants from a sure death by preventing the floor above them from collapsing. Above them, the Zero fighters returned again and again to riddle the blue ensign on Government House lawn with bullet holes.

The town's postal workers were not as fortunate. Nine people were killed instantly when the post office took a direct hit. Postmaster Hurtle Bald, who had shaken hands with Charles Kingsford Smith the day he returned with the rescued mail from Timor, was killed, along with his wife Alice and their 20-year-old daughter Iris. Also dead were four telephonists who had remained at their stations—Emily Young, Eileen and Jean Mullen and Freda Stasinowsky—their supervisor Archibald Halls, and another postal worker, Arthur Wellington. Walter Rowling, a telephone technician, later died from his injuries.

As the shattered town lay burning, a second attack began less than two hours after the first had started, with 54 Betty bombers attacking Darwin's RAAF base. It was destroyed but the loss of life was surprisingly low, with just six men killed.

A subsequent investigation into the lack of advance warning of the Japanese attack was conducted. Three-quarters of an hour before the bombing, a coastwatcher on Melville Island had spotted a large number of aircraft flying towards Darwin and contacted the naval station. Within minutes, the Catholic mission station on Bathurst Island had contacted Darwin's wireless station after also sighting the planes. But it appears these warnings were not acted on, and it is thought that, along with the residents of Darwin, the RAAF believed the approaching aircraft were American. The findings of the investigation, known as the Lowe Report, concluded:

> It is impossible to say with certainty what would have happened if the warning had been promptly given when received by the RAAF . . . but it is at least probable that a number of men who lost their lives while working on the wharf might have escaped to a place of safety . . . a twenty minutes warning might also have enabled the officials at the post office who were killed to have gone to a place of safety.

The Lowe Report found that 243 servicemen and civilians had been killed that day, although the real figure was probably higher. It is doubtful whether the death count included any Aborigines and in the ensuing evacuation of Darwin those in nearby Aboriginal settlements were left to fend for themselves.

Delfin Cubillo, a Darwin dental technician who lost his brother Juan on the wharf that day, later recounted the creation of the town's first mass grave:

> They bulldozed a big hole and all those people who were killed at the Post Office, including Hurtle Bald the Postmaster, his wife Alice and their daughter Iris, typist and women telephonists, and all the bodies that were picked up, were put in the mass grave. A lot of the bodies were washed up on Mindil Beach, and the Authorities just rolled them on to canvas and dragged them up to the high water mark as it was soft they dug a big hole and they were buried there.

The bodies were later moved to the Adelaide River War Cemetery, which was to become the resting place of 63 civilians and 434 service personnel and the largest war cemetery in Australia.

※

Some 30,000 Australians were taken prisoner in World War II, and more than two-thirds of those were held by the Japanese. In January 1942, John May was a young chaplain in the Australian Army on the Papua New Guinea island of Rabaul. Then the Japanese came. The 1400 Australian troops didn't have a chance. They were outnumbered 12 to one and the Japanese had another 7000 in reserve. According to the Australian War Memorial, in a 'brave but foredoomed action', eight Australian Wirraways challenged the advancing Japanese, but one plane crashed, three were shot down, two crash-landed and another was damaged. The Australian troops were captured, although some made it across to the other side of the island, only to be captured by the Japanese there. Some 130 of these men were subsequently rounded up and shot or bayoneted at a place called Tol Plantation. Only a handful managed to escape, with one soldier managing to survive by feigning death, despite sustaining 11 bayonet wounds.

What followed took the men by surprise. A few weeks after capture and still being held on Rabaul, Chaplain May's commanding officer informed his men that their captors had told him that if they wrote letters home, the Japanese would deliver them on a regular bombing raid. A stunned May, along with his comrades, sat down and wrote what he probably believed would be his last letter home:

My beloved family, here I am at last to write to you a few lines . . . it's wonderful to be able to. You'll never know how much I've hoped and prayed that you would know that everything is alright . . . An officer came several days ago and said that we may write and that our letters will be dropped, to use his words in place of a bomb. The Japanese are treating us very well . . . This is a pleasant spot with a lovely hibiscus avenue and roses in the garden. I am enclosing one . . . please don't worry. We've been told many times that we shall go back to Australia after the war. God bless you and keep you safe until I come home. Cheerio and all my love, Jack.

The Japanese kept their word. Amazingly, the letters got through, dropped during a raid on Port Moresby and delivered in due course to the post office.

Most of May's mates never made it home. In June 1942, more than 1000 Australian POWs were loaded onto the Japanese transport ship the *Montevideo Maru*. Just before their departure, May read them Psalm 107:

Others went out on the sea in ships;
they were merchants on the mighty waters.

They saw the works of the LORD,
his wonderful deeds in the deep.

For he spoke and stirred up a tempest
that lifted high the waves.

They mounted up to the heavens and went down to the
depths;
in their peril their courage melted away.

They reeled and staggered like drunken men;
they were at their wits' end.

Then they cried out to the LORD in their trouble,
and he brought them out of their distress.

He stilled the storm to a whisper;
the waves of the sea were hushed.

They were glad when it grew calm,
and he guided them to their desired haven.

Let them give thanks to the LORD for his unfailing love
and his wonderful deeds for men.

A legitimate Allied target, the Japanese vessel was sunk by an
American submarine and there were no survivors. The loss
of the *Montevideo Maru* remains the greatest single maritime
tragedy in Australian history.

By 1942, the cheerful congratulatory ornamental telegrams
the Post Office introduced during the Depression to encour-
age the use of the telegraph service for more than just urgent
messages appeared inappropriate. The arrival of a telegram in
wartime was invariably associated with death, serious injury
or the capture of a loved one serving abroad. Special telegram
forms were designed—white paper with the message printed

in royal purple ink. The telegrams arrived in an envelope printed with the Commonwealth coat of arms. The purple print soon became an instant warning for the recipient to expect the worst.

Doug Mitchell, a former operations supervisor and instructor for Australia Post, started his career as a telegraph boy during the war. Like many callow teenagers, his job was to deliver the worst possible news to families of Australian soldiers. Mitchell recalls that when delivering Defence Department telegrams involving service personnel being maimed or killed, the messenger had to get a signature from the recipient. Such errands were done with trepidation, knowing what the message contained.

> On one occasion I was aware it was her son who had been killed in action. I got her to sign for it and handed it to her and I paused, not really knowing how I could help her . . . She screamed and upon her screaming and holding the telegram in her hand and crying away . . . the lady that lived in the semi detached next door came out, saw that I had been the cause of her unfortunate displeasure there and she beat me all the way down the street with a millet broom.

Mitchell still remembers vividly the despair of that woman. 'And I can still feel the whacks of that millet as the lady next door belted me probably for 50 yards down the street before she returned to assist the friendly neighbour next door.'

Eventually, delivery of a telegram printed in royal purple ink bearing the Commonwealth coat of arms became the responsibility of either the postmaster or a minister of religion, and teenage boys were relieved from the harrowing duty of making the death knocks.

CHAPTER 8

POSTWAR
PROGRESS

Hello citizens. The war is over. The Japanese Government has accepted the terms of surrender imposed by the allied nations and hostilities will now cease. At this moment let us offer thanks to God.
BEN CHIFLEY, VP DAY 1945

Upon Ben Chifley's announcement at nine o'clock on Wednesday morning, 15 August 1945, six years of hardship and grief vanished in a gleeful chorus of national celebration. Hundreds of thousands of city folk converged on main streets to wave flags, frolic in ticker tape and hug strangers. And invariably the backdrop to these scenes was the GPO.

One of the hundreds of enduring images of VP Day is a photograph of a 22-year-old army medical assistant, Marjorie Boxhall, beaming outside Melbourne's GPO. 'VP Day was chaotic with the kissing and hugging . . . our boys were coming home at last,' she said in a 2005 interview with the *Herald Sun*, marking the 60th anniversary of the war in the Pacific.

In Sydney thousands dropped what they were doing and swarmed out of Martin Place's imposing sandstone buildings— the Commonwealth offices, the big banks and the GPO—to dance, kiss and weep. With its blacked-out glass roof lights and timber slats and sloped awnings covering the external sandstone to act as a pedestrian refuge, Sydney's grand old GPO had been drastically altered during the war. It had played a strategically important role, becoming a stronghold of vital communications equipment within its morse room and trunk telephone exchange. But with its tower and clock reaching almost 46 metres above the ground, there were fears the GPO could act as a beacon to hostile aircraft. After the fall of Singapore in 1942 made a Japanese invasion of Australia a very real possibility, the tower was removed stone by stone. Each block was listed, numbered and placed into storage; the stone would remain there for 20 years.

An ABC radio report of the time captured the elation of VP Day:

Hello everyone, this is Talbot Duckmanton speaking to you from Martin Place, Sydney. Honestly, I've never seen so many people in Martin Place before. There are men, women and girls, lovely girls too, hundreds and hundreds of them. They've got paper hats on their heads, waving streamers, flags, union jacks, the stars and stripes. They've got whistles, and they're just having one whale of a time.

Yes, Sydney is gay today. But I must mention that there is a little bit of sadness too. You only have to look at the cenotaph to realise that. The freshly laid flowers upon it and the number of people who have taken off their hats and reverently gone and paid homage at the cenotaph indicates to us that Sydney, despite all this gaiety and rejoicing at the news, the official news of the Japanese surrender, has not forgotten that our men and our lives too have paid a high price so that we may rejoice in this way.

According to historian Ken Inglis, a myth persists to this day about the delightfully named Talbot Duckmanton, who started at the ABC as a cadet sports reporter in 1939 and went on to become general manager of the broadcaster from 1965 to 1982. Legend has it that the ABC's GPO Box 9994 was chosen by Sir Talbot, as he later became, in honour of Don Bradman's test batting average. In fact the ABC wasn't given that address until after Duckmanton retired, Inglis points out; the GPO box had been allocated to the ABC by a postal official 'who may or may not have had Sir Donald Bradman in mind'.

Merle Storrie formerly of the Women's Royal Australian Naval Service, whose twin brother Don had been killed earlier that year, was holidaying in Sydney on VP Day:

Martin Place was packed, our hotel closed but they put on a private dinner for us . . . My sister was a nurse and the boys put her on top of the table and sang Rose of No Man's Land. They were all pretty full. But back in the room I broke down and sobbed my heart out—I'd lost Don in March.

The vast temporary workforce which had processed millions of letters, Airgraphs, parcels and telegrams stepped aside to make way for the returning troops, but many never returned to their jobs. Almost a million Australians, both men and women, played a direct role in World War II. Almost 40,000 were killed. Of the 22,000 Australians taken prisoner by the Japanese, more than a third had died in the POW camps during transportation.

Mail services quickly returned to normal. Overseas surface mail was reinstated almost immediately and by the following year, airmail was once more evolving quickly. By the late 1940s, a letter from Europe was taking as little as 10 days to arrive. Increasingly exotic destinations in Europe, Asia and Africa were added to the airmail routes, but the service still came at a premium. A half-ounce (14-gram) airmail letter to Chile, for example, cost 5 shillings and sixpence, the equivalent today of more than $10. At the same time Australia saw a kaleidoscope of cultures landing on its own doorstep through a postwar immigration boom. And with the commencement of the Snowy Mountains Hydro-electric Scheme in 1949, more than 60,000 of those migrants from more than 30 different countries would help build what today is still regarded as an engineering wonder of the modern world.

Writer and filmmaker Siobhán McHugh, who chronicled the lives of many of these migrants in her book *The Snowy— The People Behind The Power*, says the Snowy Mountains Scheme was as much a remarkable feat of social engineering as it was of scientific engineering. A 'microcosm of Europe was transplanted into the iconic wilderness of Australia's High Country, home of the fabled Man from Snowy River'.

148

The scheme saw the construction of 16 major dams, seven power stations and 145 kilometres of tunnels, all designed to turn the rivers back through the mountains so as to generate electricity and irrigate an arid heartland. Over the scheme's 25-year construction period, 121 men lost their lives. Many of those fatal accidents would have been avoided but for the hectic pace at which the workforce was driven to complete the project, says McHugh.

What was truly extraordinary about the most ambitious engineering project Australia had ever embarked upon was the fact that wartime enmities, still raw from the calamitous events of a few years earlier, were put aside. Poles and Czechs, who had suffered terribly under invasion, worked side by side with Germans, as did Serbs with Croats and Australians with Italians. Said one former German soldier interviewed by McHugh before his death: 'We wanted to show we could make something for peace too.'

The Snowy proved 'a monument to multiculturalism, mateship and endurance' and, in the words of eminent historian Manning Clark, 'an inspiration to all who dream dreams about Australia'. It also, says McHugh, marked a coming of age for Australia. 'When the Scheme started, Australia looked to the USA for technical expertise and to Britain for approbation. By the time it ended in 1974, Australia was internationally recognised for its engineering know-how and had earned its own place on the world map.'

Postwar immigration contributed to another explosion in international mail. By 1949, the Post Office was handling 1.3 billion domestic and overseas articles every year, and over the next decade, Australia would become the owner

149

of one of the largest airmail and air freight businesses in the world. The 1950s saw the PMG's Department embark on a £30 million construction program, which ranged from extending trunk and cable networks to building new post offices in the growing regional townships and burgeoning suburbs of the major cities.

Labour shortages brought on by the construction boom meant higher wages and strong trade unions, which pushed through reforms such as paid sick leave and annual leave. Having tasted the social and financial independence that came with paid employment during the war, women would never again allow themselves to be prescribed solely the roles of homemaker and child rearer, although inequalities in the workforce between male and female employees persisted. With prosperity came the aspiration of home ownership among a working class which, a generation earlier, would never have dreamt of such a thing. Modern conveniences such as the family car and the latest in household appliances, once luxuries only the very wealthy could afford, gained widespread attainability, and the cult of consumerism began.

The concept of an 'Australian way of life' developed, in part as a reactionary response to the influx of unfamiliar cultures the immigration wave had brought. Somewhat paradoxically, however, as a newly multicultural Australia sought to establish an independent national identity, the flames of affection and reverence for Britain and its beautiful young Queen needed little fanning by an effusive Prime Minister, Robert Menzies, in the lead-up to the country's first visit by a reigning monarch.

To commemorate the Royal Tour of 1954, the Post Office released special stamps, adopting Dorothy Wilding's classic

1952 portrait of a 26-year-old monarch using intaglio print in deep, regal purple. The tour would prove to be the last great pre-television event in Australia, with almost three out of four Australians—some seven million men, women and children—a lot of children—laying eyes on Queen Elizabeth II. The frenzied two-month tour cost the Australian people more than £500,000, with almost one-fifth of that figure being spent on decorations and illuminations for the 70 regional towns and all capital cities (with the exception of Darwin) the Queen was to visit. In Sydney, traffic reached gridlock before the royal party had even arrived, with 20,000 cars pouring into the city on the first evening the decorations were illuminated.

An outbreak of polio in Western Australia just weeks earlier forced the Federal Government to release pamphlets nationally. To protect the Queen and her husband, the Duke of Edinburgh, no member of the public anywhere in the country was to come within 6 feet (1.8 metres) of the royal party, while hand-shaking was definitely out of the question. The Salk vaccine for immunisation against polio would not be introduced into Australia until the following year. There was also concern that the flies might bother Her Majesty— particularly in Canberra. The government sought the expert advice of CSIRO over the problem. The mass spraying of buildings and gardens with DDT followed.

Just as Australia saw itself as being on show to Britain during the tour, the Queen was on show to Australians. Who she saw, what she said, and—most importantly—what she wore, were all reported daily in minute detail from the moment an estimated half-million people on Sydney's harbour foreshores witnessed her arrival at Farm Cove at 10.33 a.m. on 3 February.

The *Sydney Morning Herald*'s women's editor described the event:

> Her dress was simplicity itself, a flutter of champagne chiffon printed in gold which had a tinge of green ... Her little hat was a pretty conceit which showed her softly waved hair ... The Queen's complexion is flawless, and paler than the impression gained from paintings and colour photographs. Many a suntanned woman yesterday must have regretted the extra hours on the beach.

The Australian people had responded to their Queen with what Menzies described as 'the most profound and passionate feelings of loyalty and devotion'. The Prime Minister wrote of the tour:

> It does not require much imagination to realise that when eight million people spontaneously pour out this feeling they are engaging in a great act of common allegiance and common joy which brings them closer together and is one of the most powerful elements converting them from a mass of individuals to a great cohesive nation. In brief, the common devotion to the Throne is a part of the very cement of the whole social structure.

Yet such fulsome expressions of loyalty came at a time when Australia was forging greater political and economic ties with a new superpower. As Australian troops headed to Korea, the ANZUS Treaty of 1951 gave Australia assurances that should the South Pacific come under military threat again, it would be the United States, not Britain, which would come to the rescue. The perceived threat of a 'yellow peril' was further addressed with the formation of the South-East Asia Treaty Organisation (SEATO) the following year. The fear Menzies whipped up over the communist threat from both Asia and Australia itself (most notably from within the Labor Party and trade unions) was not strong enough to outlaw the Communist Party, as he tried to do in 1951, but the ensuing Petrov Affair and the subsequent Royal Commission on Espionage ensured Australia would not be free from escalating Cold War tensions throughout the 1950s.

As Soviet tanks rolled into Budapest, Melbourne was just a month off opening the 1956 Olympic Games. Widespread scepticism of Australia's ability to stage the games challenged the sense of national self-affirmation the Royal Tour had generated just two years earlier. Venue construction had been slow, largely through industrial unrest, and Melbourne's apparent lack of sophistication—from its six o'clock swill to the insistence Sunday remain sacred (and therefore a day of rest for the Olympians)—drew criticism and some derision. Yet these problems were trifling compared to the political backdrop to the games. In protest over the invasion of Hungary, the Netherlands, Spain and Switzerland pulled out, while escalating hostilities against Egypt by Britain and France over the Suez Canal saw the non-participation of Lebanon and Iraq. In protest over Taiwan's participation as a nation in its own right, the People's Republic of China also withdrew.

The Melbourne Olympics made heroes of Betty Cuthbert, Dawn Fraser and Murray Rose, all of whom would later be immortalised in Australia Post stamps. But the many countries' absence at the opening ceremony on 22 November caused some to express fears that Melbourne 1956 might signal the end of the Olympic's age of innocence. When blood flowed in the water polo pool at the semi-final between the Soviet Union and Hungary two weeks later, all doubt was removed.

As well as this turmoil, there was a stand-off between the IOC and a new electronic medium already flexing its muscles. Television had arrived in Australia. Official broadcasting had begun only a month before the Olympics opening ceremony and the country had just 5000 television sets to show for it. The assumption by television of its right to free access to a world event jarred with the IOC's determination to establish a principle of payment for rights from the outset.

The phenomenon of television affected the Post Office directly. As it had already been given the duty of supervising civil radio stations and issuing licences to radio listeners, it fell to the Post Office to issue licences and receive payments for television ownership, a role it continued to perform until licences were abolished in 1974.

By the end of the 1950s, the Post Office had a full-time workforce of 86,000 staff and an additional 15,000 non-official staff. According to the PMG's 1958/59 annual report, there were over 17,000 postal and telegraph facilities across the country, collectively handling almost two billion articles a year. Annual turnover exceeded £928 million.

On 1 November 1959, the PMG announced that the long-standing domestic airmail surcharge of threepence would be abolished. For the majority of Australians who now had access to air services, a standard domestic letter would receive airmail carriage free of additional charges. It had been just 30 years since Qantas carried its first airmail from Charleville to Brisbane.

Marking the 150th anniversary since Isaac Nichols took charge of the first bag of mail on Sydney's wharves, the *Sydney Morning Herald* paid tribute to a vast organisation's postmasters and postmistresses, postal clerks and posties, telegraphists and telephonists, and myriad technicians, engineers and mail sorters: 'The click of a mailbox, the shrill of a whistle and another letter has found its way to the person to whom it is addressed . . . Behind that arrival is a vast organisation the ramifications of which are unknown to most people.'

❊

Fifty years after Maurice Guillaux delivered the first mail by aeroplane from Melbourne to Sydney, more than 100 domestic airmail services were criss-crossing the country. In addition, more than 2000 tonnes of mail left Australia's shores each year, the bulk of it carried by Qantas. Innovations in speed were needed to keep the ever-increasing volumes of mail moving. The processing of letters and parcels entered the age of mechanisation, with sorting machines and conveyor belts moving into the mail exchanges in the capital cities. In 1962, Melbourne's city workers queued to use Australia's first automatic postal station, while businesses welcomed the introduction of postage paid labels.

With mechanisation came centralisation. In 1965, the world's largest automated mail coding and sorting plant opened in the inner-city Sydney suburb of Redfern. Two years later, the seven-storey Sydney Mail Exchange became the first mail centre in Australia to sort mail automatically by postcode. No longer would automatic sorting machines have to 'read' the alphabetical data and distinguish between Meckering, Meekatharra, Merkanooka and Mooliabeene; all the machine needed to do was recognise four numbers in sequence.

Every city, town, suburb and rural area was issued with a four-digit postcode, and the allocation system was as ingenious as it was simple. The first digit of the postcode corresponded with the call sign of each state's radio station—for example 3LO in Victoria and 2BL in New South Wales. The other three digits were allocated starting from the capital cities' centres (Sydney CBD being 2000 and 2001) then progressing across the suburbs from west to north and east to south, subsequently followed by regional and rural areas. To allow for suburban sprawl on the outskirts of major cities, some postcodes were kept in reserve.

There was one core function of the postal services which did not continue to prosper, however. In mid-1963, the final morse telegram tapped its way into retirement. The days of the telegraph boy were over, and no longer was proficiency in morse code a prerequisite for career advancement in the Post Office. Manual transmission was replaced by automatic teleprinters, with the PMG's development of TRESS—the teleprinter reperforator switching system. But even before this innovation was introduced, Australians' love affair with the telegram had ended, largely because of the vast strides made in airmail services and trunk line facilities throughout the 1950s and 60s.

The way in which Australians communicated was changing dramatically. The 5000 television sets which had switched on to the Melbourne Olympics in 1956 had multiplied at a staggering rate. At the end of the 1950s, it was estimated that less than 5 per cent of the residents in Melbourne, and fewer than 1 per cent in Sydney owned a television set. By the end of the 1960s, over 90 per cent of Australian homes in accessible areas possessed such a thing. The Vietnam War, and the increasingly strident protests against Australia's involvement in it, played out in people's living rooms nightly, as did the mystery of a prime minister lost at sea, the official recognition of the country's indigenous people through referendum, and man's first steps on the moon. All the while, the ties that bound the dominion to its mother country continued to loosen. As Britain entered Europe's Common Market, Australia looked to its former wartime enemy and found a lucrative export market in Japan. In little more than a decade, a nation's 'profound and passionate feelings of loyalty and devotion' to the monarchy had dissipated to the point that when the government announced the new decimal currency was to be called the 'royal', such was the public outcry the term 'dollar' had to be adopted instead.

The pence to cents transition was a major undertaking for the Post Office, requiring the conversion of all its vending and stamping machines, along with the reprinting of all stamps. Two days before the decimal conversion, post offices withdrew all pre-decimal stamps from sale. On 14 February 1966, more than 250,000 letters were postmarked, with philatelists eager to get their first-day covers.

The Post Office had become a monolithic beast, upon whose shoulders virtually all forms of communication rested. It ran the entire nation's postal and telegraphic systems, issued licences to the millions of owners of radios and televisions in the country, served as a conduit for the paying of war pensions, age and disability pensions, child endowment payments, and in turn collected for the government, with facilities for receiving War Service Homes repayments and state stamp duties. In addition, the Post Office operated as a surrogate bank. By the 1960s, its relationship with the Commonwealth Bank, which had begun in 1916, had spread to almost 5000 post offices across the country. Today, the CBA's 3800 Australia Post agencies still outnumber the 3200 automatic teller machines the bank operates nationally.

But postal and other services were being rapidly overtaken in importance by telephony. Since that first faint message was sent down an experimental 10-kilometre wire in 1854, the popularity of the telegram had grown unabatedly, peaking at 35 million a year in 1946. By 1959, however, that figure was dwarfed by the 1295 million telephone conversations the Post Office's exchanges were connecting in a single year.

According to the Australian Heritage Council, the first installation of a regular telephone service in Australia was as early as 1878, when the Melbourne firm of Messrs McLean Brothers and Rigg connected their Elizabeth Street head office with their Spencer Street office about a kilometre away. The first government telephone exchange opened at Sydney's GPO in 1882, although by then a private operator known as the Sydney Royal Exchange was already operating Australia's first switchboard. But a thunderstorm caused an electrical short circuit which burnt out the private switchboard, and in 1883, rather than face the costly exercise of acquiring a new switchboard to service its 30 subscribers, the company handed its business over to the Post Office. The precedent for government control of telephonic services was established, with other colonies soon following.

Unlike the telegraph system, however, at the time of Federation Australia still lacked any significant interstate or any overseas telephone services, as the colonies had each developed their connections in isolation. The Todd Inquiry of 1901 recorded that Australia's population of 3.3 million was served by 116 exchanges, 24,708 telephone lines and 32,767 telephones connected. In other words, fewer than one in a hundred Australians owned a telephone. Six years later, the first Sydney to Melbourne telephone line was opened. It was capable of handling only about 40 calls per day and the charge was 6 shillings per minute. In today's terms, a five-minute interstate chat on the telephone would have cost the subscriber well over $100. The prohibitive costs of the telephone compared to the increasingly affordable telegraphic services meant that even up until World War II, most people preferred to communicate between the two cities by telegram rather than telephone. Nevertheless, the popularity of the telephone grew and by the late 1930s a mass market in local telephone calls was established.

Although the first overseas telephone calls were made in 1930, operator-assisted international calls would not commence for another 33 years, and then only to Canada, the United States and Britain. However, by 1956, the introduction of a crossbar exchange gave Australians Subscriber Trunk Dialling (STD), allowing interstate calls to be made as easily as local calls. An efficient national telephone system had arrived, and by 1970, a broadband system stretching 11,200 kilometres across the country was delivering multi-circuited, high-capacity communication.

With all these developments the Post Office had become the country's largest business, controlling all postal and tele-communications services across Australia. Yet as Marcella Hunter points out in her history of postal services, the fundamental problem was that the Post Office was really two different organisations, each with different workforces and management requirements. There was no denying that by the late 1940s, these two organisations had switched places. The once profitable postal service, which had bankrolled the costly roll-out of an increasingly sophisticated telecommunications system, was now being subsidised by that very same system.

When the Australian Labor Party swept into power in 1972 ending 23 years of coalition government, it took less than three months for the Whitlam Government to call for a full-scale investigation into Australian postal and telecommunications services. The 18-month inquiry was to be chaired by Sir James Vernon, and the appointment in itself was significant. Eight years earlier Vernon had delivered a wide-ranging government-commissioned report on Australian postwar economic policy and how future growth might be encouraged. The report's main recommendation—that an independent group of economic policy advisers be established—had been dismissed by Menzies, on the advice of Treasury, which understandably saw such a move as a threat. Vernon's report was, nevertheless, to give rise to the National Economic Summit and the Economic Planning Advisory Commission. The second Vernon Inquiry was to examine the competing demands of the country's postal and telecommunications services, and propose changes to the organisation's administration and operation.

Almost 500 submissions were received by the inquiry. The Post Office's operations affected almost all aspects of Australian life, from the political to the private, from the community to the commercial, and the diversity of submissions reflected the wide-ranging and vital role the organisation had within Australian society. The Australian Post Office's own submission came to a hefty six volumes. While within its pages the pros and cons of splitting the competing postal and telecommunications services were discussed, the organisation stopped short of making recommendations for its own future.

The commission presented its findings to the government in mid-1974. 'Each of the services is a large and important enterprise in its own right,' the report concluded, 'and the time has come to place them under separate administration.'

The unanimous recommendation to establish two statutory authorities surprised no one. With a divestiture date less than 12 months away, the newly named Australian Postal Commission—trading as Australia Post—and the Australian Telecommunications Commission—trading as Telecom Australia—began immediate preparations for an amicable divorce. And inevitably, splitting up the assets would prove one of the biggest challenges.

Many of the country's post offices were home to both postal and telephone services, particularly in the country's small towns and regional centres. Unless a new home could be found for either, cohabitation was the only option, operating on a complex system of leasing. If Australia Post retained a piece of real estate, then Telecom had to pay rent, and vice versa. Telecom Australia got to keep the 'family home'—Melbourne's head office. Australia Post packed its bags and moved into temporary accommodation until its new headquarters in Rathdowne Street, Melbourne, were completed.

In terms of human resources, the scale of the split had been enormous. The transformation from ageing bureaucracy to two separate statutory bodies halved the Commonwealth public service overnight. Reflecting the labour-intensive operation telecommunications had become by the mid-1970s, three-quarters of the workforce went to Telecom.

'It was an enormous task, dividing up 120,000 people,' Australia Post's first chairman, James Kennedy, told Hunter. 'But it was not about eliminating jobs. It was a revolutionary process in terms of the Commonwealth setting up statutory bodies.'

The Postmaster-General's Department became the Postal and Telecommunications Department, and Australia Post was expected to operate independently, reporting directly to the minister. After generations of government subsidy, the new statutory body was also expected to cover its own operating costs, along with funding at least half of its capital expenditure.

From the first overseas telegrams of the 1870s to the first airmail services of the 20th century, history had shown Australia Post that Australians were prepared to pay a premium for progress in postal services. And it was innovations such as the next-day interstate Priority Paid service and the Australia Post Courier interstate service which enabled Australia Post to exceed its break-even brief and record a trading surplus for nine of its first 10 years of operation.

Not all the changes the new financially independent organisation introduced were popular, however. Just two months after divestiture, the basic postage rate rose from 10 cents to 18 cents. Telecom Australia raised its charge for a local call from 6 cents to 9. Some members of the public did not take too kindly to the new user-pays system and Kennedy admits Australia Post weathered some pretty tough criticism from the public and the press over the price hike, including from one irate elderly woman who recognised him in the street. 'You ought to be ashamed of yourself, young man!' she berated him, shaking her umbrella.

To prime the public on the independent new Australia Post and Telecom Australia entities, an advertising campaign had been launched leading up to divestiture day. The Post Office had embraced television advertising some years earlier, often using a young Fred Schepisi and his Melbourne-based Film House company to create imaginative and humorous campaigns. A year after the big separation in the PMG's Department, Schepisi would be directing his first feature film, *The Devil's Playground*. With the slogan 'keeping pace with the changing times', television viewers soon became accustomed to the new titles attached to their postal and telecommunications services. Irony aside, keeping pace with the changing times meant taking a step back to the future for Australia Post. The new organisation was returning to the original core business Isaac Nichols had begun almost 170 years earlier: getting the mail through.

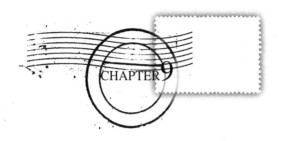

STAMPS OF A NEW
AUSTRALIA

With a flash of gold lamé and the flick of a psychedelic tie, the last vestiges of the White Australia Policy were swept away by the Whitlam Government. On 11 August 1973, a sartorially splendid Minister for Immigration, Al Grassby, delivered his policy speech, 'A Multi-Cultural Society for the Future', and a new word entered the Australian vernacular. Less than 20 years earlier, as Australia celebrated the arrival of its millionth migrant, such a concept as multiculturalism would have been unthinkable. Utterly in keeping with Australia's pro-British immigration mindset, when the country feted its millionth postwar migrant, she happened to be a 21-year-old Englishwoman who looked like the young Queen Elizabeth—and was treated accordingly.

To celebrate the millionth migrant, the Menzies Government agreed that a special stamp was in order, and migrants were asked to offer their ideas. The Department of Immigration and the Postmaster-General would spend the next three years arguing over it. According to the National Museum of Australia, postwar migration publicity campaigns were marked by the achievement of numerical targets, and chance had little to do with finding the millionth migrant. Individuals were carefully chosen by departmental officials to present an ideologically attractive face of migration to the Australian public.

Barbara Porritt, a newly married 21-year-old from Yorkshire, was the perfect migrant. She was pretty, white and skilled— a stenographer—and her young husband Dennis, was an electrical fitter, who upon arrival would walk straight into a job with Victoria's State Electricity Commission. More importantly, the Porritts' youth and essential 'British-ness' epitomised the ideal of quality breeding stock in a country whose non-indigenous, native-born population was still enormously ambivalent about the social and cultural changes the postwar immigration wave had brought.

The Porritts were to become a vital cog in the government's propaganda machine. Their quiet hometown wedding in Red-car prior to departure was covered by Australian newspapers. The Minister for Immigration, Harold Holt, had even sent the couple a congratulatory telegram, assuring them on behalf of nine million 'prospective good neighbours', they would receive a warm welcome in their new country. Holt also reminded Mrs Porritt she had:

been chosen to carry the title of Australia's millionth migrant because we see you as the most fitting representative of the first million settlers of this period . . . and because, with your husband, you typify the kind of migrant we hope will follow you in even greater numbers . . . May the success and contentment which are yours for the asking in Australia continue enduringly for you the happiness of your wedding day.

The Porritts were among 307 British migrants on board the *Oronsay*, and according to *The Age*, by the voyage's end on 8 November 1955, 'our girl in a million' was feeling more than a little nervous over all the fuss, and confided as much to the ship's captain.

> Though accompanied by the husband who had convinced her that 'Australia offers you everything', Mrs Porritt appreciated the reassurance of the Captain at what had been planned as a dinner of welcome. Gallantly, Captain Burnand put her mind at ease by putting his arm around her and planting a kiss on her cheek. Australian Minister for Immigration, Harold Holt, who was also at the dinner, immediately leapt to his feet and shook the Captain's hand, congratulating him for 'doing what everyone else had wanted to do to her as soon as they saw her'.

When the couple moved into their modest home in Yallourn, the media ensured that Mrs Porritt was literally carried across the threshold. There she would remain, it was suggested—the young wife readying herself to nurture a fresh generation of little Australians—while her breadwinner husband went out in the world to contribute to society.

In fact, Mrs Porritt went quietly out to work herself, although that was never part of the propaganda.

Meanwhile, the design for the commemorative millionth migrant stamp was not progressing well. The Postmaster-General had rejected a design by Melbourne artist Ralph Warner, which bore the motto 'Migration: Aid to Progress' and depicted a giant wheel of industry supported by two muscular male workers. Another design was submitted to the government, only to be rejected by Holt himself. A competition to design a stamp 'significant of post-war immigration to Australia' was announced. Some 300 entries were received but no decision on a winner was made. According to the Australia Post publication *Stamping the Nation*, the subject of the stamp reappeared intermittently on the Stamp Advisory Committee's agenda in 1957 and 1958. But then it appeared to lapse.

By this time, the fuss over Barbara and Dennis Porritt had settled down and the couple were starting a family of young Australians. They went on to dutifully provide the country with three daughters and five grandchildren.

The striking resemblance of Mrs Porritt to the young Queen Elizabeth, whose visit had prompted mass euphoria just a year earlier, no doubt contributed to the warm welcome some nine million new good neighbours did indeed extend to Australia's millionth migrant. But the altercation over the commemorative stamp to mark the milestone hadn't been the Post Office's first controversy, nor would it be the last, particularly when it came to the role a British monarch's head should play.

Following Federation, Queensland and New South Wales decided to road test a stamp depicting Britannia with state seals around her as a prototype Australian stamp; King Edward VII was nowhere to be seen. Someone back in Britain wasn't amused, particularly as it was the press which broke the news. On 16 July 1903, Joseph Chamberlain, Secretary of State for the Colonies, sent a cable to Prime Minister Edmund Barton: 'Press messages it is proposed new Commonwealth stamp should not bear head of King. Hope report unfounded as His Majesty desires that his head appear on all stamps.' 'Noted' was Prime Minister Barton's succinct response. The government in Melbourne yielded, however, sending assurances to its colonial masters that any general stamp adopted by Australia would indeed bear the King's head. The controversy was the forerunner of many a republican debate to come.

By 1911, Australia still had no Commonwealth stamp. A competition was called for, with stipulations the design 'must contain features characteristic of Australia'. More than 1000 entries were submitted and a winner duly chosen. Herman Altmann from Victoria collected the £100 prize money for his ornate portrait of George V, flanked by emu, kangaroo, crown and each of the six states' emblems.

The new Postmaster-General, Labour's Charles Frazer (the party was not to drop the 'u' until the following year, in a nod to the American labor movement), described Altmann's stamp design as 'execrable'. At 30 years and four months of age, Frazer was the youngest politician to be appointed to a Federal Government ministry, a record unbroken for almost a century (until Kate Ellis, at the age of 30 years and three months, was appointed Minister for Sport and Youth by Prime Minister Kevin Rudd in late 2007). Frazer was a former engine driver

and goldminer whose father had witnessed the Eureka Stockade. The man who was already being tipped as prime ministerial
material wanted something quintessentially Australian, and
he openly declared a preference for 'a picturesque stamp . . . in
which an outline of Australia is a feature'.

The competition's judges had named two second prize-
winners, one of whom was a London gentleman called
Edwin Arnold. Under the nom de plume 'Baldy', he had
submitted a simple design of a standing kangaroo. Frazer,
who according to his online biographer Ross McMullin,
was privately contemptuous of the postal service's senior
employees, describing them as 'unreasonable', 'far too well
paid' and like 'spoilt children', issued them a brief: 'Get
coastline of Australia; insert Baldy's Roo; produce in colours
for different denominates.'

Australia's first Commonwealth stamp was put on show
to the public on 2 April 1912, and the reaction was one of
immediate outrage. The concept of placing an 'absurd' animal
on a national stamp was ludicrous to some; the tufts of grass
which sprouted at the marsupial's feet like a pair of rabbit's
ears only seemed to add to the comical tone. Australia had
become 'the laughing stock of civilised countries', appalled
critics warned. Others objected to the stamp's simplicity,
which was uncharacteristic of the era, while a cartoon in
Sydney's *Daily Telegraph* suggested the 'wasteland overrun by
the kangaroo' was reminiscent of the seven-year drought the
country had endured only a few years earlier. Worst of all,
however, was the fact that the stamp gave no indication, let
alone paid reverence, to the British monarchy. An editorial
in the *Argus* on 4 April 1912, stated: 'Even if Mr Frazer

entertains Republican sentiments and thinks it is his duty to express them by means of the national stamp he might surely have found some heraldic device more noble and dignified than that absurd Kangaroo.'

When news travelled back to London, the monarch was taken aback by the insolence of its largest dominion. According to philatelist Glen Stephens, King George V was a man who took his stamp collecting seriously—something his wife Queen Mary appeared eternally grateful for. When asked once about her husband's hobby, she replied: 'It keeps him out of mischief' (which may or may not have been a veiled reference to George's father, Edward VII, a notorious collector of women). In World War I, when troops were dying by the thousands on the Somme, the British Prime Minister, Herbert Asquith, would patiently wait outside the war room, not daring to interrupt George as he perused his impressive stamp collection.

Frazer stood firm. The brazen stamp stayed, much to the chagrin of many a newspaper editorial. The *Daily Telegraph* for one maintained the rage, writing on 13 January 1913: 'The kangaroo be it observed replaces the head of His Majesty, a result which is likely to arouse in the outside world dubious speculations if not as to the loyalty or at any rate as to the good taste of this part of the King's dominions.' In June 1913, the Labor Government lost power, and the new Postmaster-General, Agar Wynne, ordered the immediate removal of the offending stamps. By decree, the King's head was back on all Australian mail.

Six months later, Frazer joined the notorious racing identity John Wren for a day at the Sydney races. He caught a severe cold and died of pneumonia three days later. He was just 33. But the man whose life was later described by a political opponent as 'brilliant' but 'spoilt by too quick success and too much leisure' was not defeated entirely in death. The national recall of his stamps was never completed. War broke out the following year, followed by another change of government, then another war. In 1948, a 2-shilling stamp bearing Baldy's roo and a map of Australia was still hopping around the country. Agar Wynne should have known how hard it could be to catch a kangaroo.

Matters of taste were not the only factors contributing to a decade-long delay in the release of Australia's first Commonwealth stamp. The position of Postmaster-General had changed hands 10 times in as many years of the Commonwealth Government's existence. With each succession, any proposals on the table for a Commonwealth stamp were promptly scrapped, and the process would begin again. To complicate the issue, under the new Constitution it was mandated that the states should receive all surplus revenue accumulated by Commonwealth departments which had previously been under state control. Once a single stamp covered the entire country, calculating each state's postal revenue promised to be a giant bookkeeping headache for the PMG's most senior public servant, Robert Townley Scott. Moreover, Scott foresaw a similar problem if the department moved to allow existing colonial stamps to be interchangeable between states.

Commercial interests were also at stake. A Commonwealth stamp would require a centralised printing headquarters, but at Federation, large printing companies were operating in four of the country's six states. This dilemma was ultimately resolved with a compromise: Victoria would print the stamps, while New South Wales would print the telephone books.

It was not until 13 October 1910 that legislative reforms permitted colonial stamps to be used throughout the country. This was one of Scott's final achievements before retiring in exasperation three months later. Six months after Scott's departure, the department achieved the goal it had been working towards for more than a decade: universal penny postage. This had been an old sore among Australians outside of Victoria, who had all been paying twopence for their half-ounce (14-gram) letters. Penny postage had been a fact of life for residents of the southern state for more than a decade.

As early as 1875, when the New South Wales postal service introduced the novelty of stamp-printed postcards at a penny each, the very existence of the twopence letter came under threat, at least for the purposes of quick local communication. On the first day of sale, 12,000 of the large decorative cards had been posted, and their low cost and speed ensured their longevity. By 1883, reply postcards with a penny stamp on each half, allowing the recipient to detach the blank half and send an immediate prepaid response, had become all the rage. Of course, privacy of correspondence was sacrificed in the exercise and postal authorities were obliged at point-of-sale to warn customers that if their card contained anything of 'an obscene, libellous or otherwise obviously objectionable nature, it may be detained or destroyed'.

By the time of Federation, Sydney was enjoying up to three mail deliveries a day, and reply postcards were the fastest means of written communication other than the telegram—and a lot cheaper. For instant communication, only the telephone could beat the service, and there weren't many domestic telephones in Sydney in 1901.

The twopenny states took as much advantage of the new penny postage rates as possible. On the day the new charges took effect, accusations of hoarding grew as the mountain of mail swelled. 'The bags resembled in bulkiness the Christmas mails,' *The Age* reported, as Melbourne's GPO was inundated with letters from interstate. 'Plainly many businessmen had accumulated their postage during the last few days to get the benefits of the reductions.'

The one-penny charge didn't just apply to letters within Australia. With regular airmail services still some three decades off, a penny could send a half-ounce letter anywhere in the British Empire, including Britain, Canada, India, South Africa and New Zealand.

'Hearty congratulations to Australia on the introduction of penny postage,' cabled New Zealand's Prime Minister Sir Joseph Ward on the first day of operations, perhaps not without a slight hint of smugness. Like Victorians, New Zealanders had enjoyed universal penny postage since 1 January 1901 and had achieved reciprocal recognition of their penny post throughout the British Empire—with the exception of Australia. Britain also welcomed the belated Australian move, with Postmaster-General Herbert Samuel wiring to his equivalent in the dominion his belief that the introduction of penny post would 'draw closer the bonds of kinship'.

❋

While still a penal colony, New South Wales had set a precedent for dropping the monarch's head right from the start. Australia's very first stamp, which was to become known by collectors much later as the 'Sydney Views', featured the figure of Hope seated on a bale of wheat overlooking Sydney Harbour. With allegorical symbols for industry and commerce in the background, it is believed the intent behind the stamp, issued in 1850, was to exhort convicts to reform. Thus Sydney Views set a precedent for the use of stamps and postmarks as inspiration—and invariably as propaganda—which would continue well into the 20th century.

During the Great Depression, slogans such as 'Give Employment—Assist National Recovery' and 'Australian Products are Excellent' appeared on postmarks across the country. Some 20 years later, Australians would be urged by their stamps to 'produce, produce, produce!'—assisted by rudimentary illustrations of beef, butter and wheat. The stamps were an embarrassment.

According to stamp specialist Geoff Kellow, the Post Office wasn't too keen on the idea from the start, but Menzies was adamant and had also set a tight deadline. The designs were hastily completed and when the stamps were released in February 1953, collectors were appalled. Brisbane philatelist Charles Dunn wrote to the *Australian Stamp Monthly* to express his dismay:

I am ashamed to be sending you the new Food stamps; yes heartily ashamed of the Australian Post Office for issuing such horrible examples of cheap job printing. They say 'Produce, Produce, Produce!'. Why did not the Post Office produce some decent stamps? They have done so in the past, but not this time. Many matchbox labels are miles better than these atrocities. They are supposed to be propaganda stamps. They are a shoddy job which will probably get a shoddy reply from the farmers.

Towards the close of each year, a panoply of Christian lobby groups, from Call to the People of Australia to the National Catholic Girls' Movement, would urge the PMG to 'put Christ back into Christmas' and issue stamps with suitably religious themes. In 1957, with the communist threat intensifying and the Soviet Union celebrating the successful launch of a dog into space in Sputnik 2, the PMG finally relented. Joshua Reynolds' portrait of a kneeling child praying established Australia as the first country in the world to regularly issue Christmas stamps. The tradition remains today, with more overt recognitions of Christmas gradually taking hold.

In 1990, the perennial question of good taste was raised when Australia Post released a stamp depicting a nativity scene, complete with adoring koala and kangaroo hovering over the infant Jesus. But nothing could compare to the uproar which erupted some 13 festive seasons earlier, when Australia Post issued the notorious 'Surfing Santa'. Richard McClade of Oak Park, Victoria, wrote to Australia Post:

The Christmas stamp for 1977 depicting a buffoon-like Father Christmas on a surfboard is a disgrace to Australia as a Christian nation. What induced the Post Office to depart from its usual custom of depicting something of the Christian significance of Christmas to providing this piece of ockerism? While other countries had Christmas stamps reproducing great works of art on the Nativity, all Australia can produce is this bibulous frivolity. I shall not use this stamp as it is an insult to the true significance of Christmas and I know that many people will do likewise. I urge you most strongly to have it withdrawn from sale as I know that many people, like myself, are incensed by it.

Well, it was the 1970s, after all, argues Noel Leahy, Australia Post's Group Manager Philatelic. He admits Surfing Santa polarised the community. 'There were those that loved it, thought it was quite funky . . . but there were the more traditionalists and they made quite a bit of noise, so it was a bit of embarrassment.'

The Surfing Santa had been intended for international mail only, and had received an acceptable response in an earlier poll conducted among various religious groups. The trade-off had been an abstract Madonna and Child by local artist Jackie O'Brien for the 15-cent domestic mail stamp. But for reasons still unclear, the two were switched at the last minute and the ruckus ensued. From the days of Baldy's roo onwards, once Australians acquired a taste for publicly critiquing their national stamps, they never really lost it. And by 1977, Australia Post management had become used to it.

Cartoon-style stamps had made their debut in Australia four years prior to the Surfing Santa scandal. In 1973, the country was in the grip of a conversion crisis. Metrics were on the way in, and Australia Post, happy to help out in the public education campaign, agreed to issue some edifying stamps. 'The Blob' was born.

Stamp designers Bruce Weatherhead and Alex Stitt had intended the large shapeless cartoon character to represent the 'average Australian', humorously demonstrating the metric equivalents to the familiar old empirical measurements. 'Bloody awful' was the way one letter to a newspaper described the stamps. The stamps would do 'untold damage to Australia's image overseas' wrote another. The concerns which had first plagued a young nation when a monarch's head was replaced by a kangaroo 60 years earlier were to be a recurring phenomenon. Just what would Britain (and other more 'sophisticated' countries) think of us? As another critic put it: 'Australia has really convinced the rest of the world it is the land of "the weird mob".'

Criticism of the metric stamps came from some unexpected quarters. The New South Wales Temperance Alliance raised strong objections to one particular stamp in the series depicting 'The Blob' converting a 7-fluid-ounce drink to 200 millilitres. The liquid in the glass looked suspiciously like beer.

Australia Post has resiliently held on to its sense of humour and fun, nonetheless. In May 2007, the philatelic department issued a limited edition of 10,000 souvenir stamp sheets celebrating an institution generations of young Australians have delighted in: cartoons. Porky Pig, Bugs Bunny, Tweety Pie, Pepe Le Pew and a host of other beloved Looney Tunes characters featured on the stamps, and failed to raise a murmur from the critics.

Errors of taste, perceived or otherwise, are one thing; errors in production are another, and as philatelists the world over know, an inadvertent printing glitch can add tens of thousands of dollars to a stamp's worth. The most famous Australian example of this is, of course, Western Australia's very first stamp. In a bold mood similar to New South Wales', the western colony did the unthinkable in 1854, overlooking a human queen for a queenly animal. The first one-penny Black Swan stamps were printed in England, but with the clipper ships of the 1850s still taking well over two months to reach Australia, urgency demanded additional denominations for the stamp be printed locally. When transferring the original swan motif to a new plate bearing higher denominations, the government lithographer accidentally flipped one of the frames upside down. Today, the single inverted swan stamp can fetch in excess of $80,000 at auction.

In an *Australian Financial Review* article of October 2007, journalist Terry Ingram pondered whether 'Australia Post's newfound accuracy' might actually be accentuating the value of its past errors. In September 2007, a 1965 five-penny stamp known within collecting circles as 'the flesh omitted' was expecting to fetch around $2500 at its forthcoming Stanley Gibbons auction. The Christmas stamp—in which the excessive paleness of Joseph and Mary is attributed to the accidental omission of brown ink in the printing process— fetched almost four times its expected price, the renowned stamp collector Arthur Gray paying $9635 for it. Earlier that year, the health food chain magnate had sold his extensive collection of Australian kangaroo stamps in New York for $8 million.

In the same month, a pair of South Australian one-penny stamps missing the 'one penny' denomination and doing King George V the great indignity of placing his head upside down, sold for $10,000 at a Prestige Philately auction in Melbourne. 'Recent improvements in security mean the bonanzas attaching to such stamps are now virtually unknown,' observed Ingram.

'If there are any errors these days, the sheets on which they are printed do not leave the printing plant.'

When an unfavourable reception is anticipated, some stamp designs in the past have never made it as far as the printing plant, most notably a 1982 design by Brett Whiteley. The celebrated and controversial artist had been commissioned to design a stamp to commemorate the 50th anniversary of the opening of the Sydney Harbour Bridge. The Post Office rejected Whiteley's effort, or as they say in the business, the design was 'unadopted'. Drawings from the original plans and photographs of the incomplete bridge were the only resources the stamp designers had to work with when creating the original stamps to celebrate the bridge's opening. On 19 March 1932, those attending the opening ceremony found temporary post offices set up in the pylons at each end of the bridge. Over the ensuing fortnight, some 60,000 letters and postcards would be processed in the granite towers, each bearing the postmark message, 'Posted on bridge during opening celebrations'. According to Australia Post's *Stamping the Nation*, the twopenny Harbour Bridge stamp, along with its contemporary George V stamp of identical denomination, were both the subject of a major forgery that year. The fake stamps were used to mail tickets, which were also forged, to an Irish sweepstakes lottery. The forgers were exposed by a 'sharp-eyed philatelist', the culprits arrested and the illegal stock seized. Such a large-scale attempt to defraud the postal services had been unprecedented.

Many Australian artists have fared better than Whiteley with their philatelic contributions. A fascination with the outback compelled Sidney Nolan many times to hitch a ride on the mail planes of the postwar period. The artist, celebrated for his Ned Kelly and Burke and Wills series, wrote in his diary from Alice Springs on 28 June 1949:

> Today went on a mail flight for four hundred miles [640 kilometres] over the Hartz Range & to the eastern extremity of the McDonnell Ranges. It is a simple matter to trace in this old waterless and eroded surface of the earth the dreaming nature and philosophy of the Aborigines . . . Transparent & at the same time impenetrable, a fitting paradox for those who would look long at it and attempt to look through it to the coloured rocks and hills themselves.

Along with Nolan, notable Australian artists whose work has featured on stamps include Tom Roberts, Fred McCubbin, Charles Condor, Joy Hester, Howard Arkley, John Glover and Arthur Streeton. In 1996, Grace Cossington Smith, who had died some years before, managed to achieve what Whiteley had not: a stamp with one of her works commemorating the construction of the Sydney Harbour Bridge. Indigenous art has been a distinctive feature of Australian stamps since 1971, with works included by Albert Namatjira, Robert Cole, Fiona Foley, Hector Jandany, George Malibirr, Ginger Riley, Tim Leura Tjapaltjarri, Rover Thomas, Jack Wunuwun and Yirawala.

A host of other prominent figures in the arts world have featured over the years, including Henry Lawson, who was celebrated in a stamp in 1949. It would take another 26 years for his mother Louisa Lawson—publisher, mother of women's suffrage and designer of a postal services buckle for fastening mail bags—to receive the same honour.

Given the national obsession with sport, however, it was inevitable that the first living Australian to feature on a stamp would be a sportsman. The long-standing custom of excluding all living persons other than the reigning British monarch from becoming subjects of stamps was not broken until 1997, when Australia Post Managing Director Graeme John suggested it was time for living role models to be celebrated on stamps. The result was what has come to be known as the Australian Legends series. And the first famous Australian to be featured in the series also proved to be its most popular. The 1997 Sir Donald Bradman stamp remains one of the highest selling stamps in Australia Post history.

Numerous Australian sportsmen and sportswomen have followed in Bradman's footsteps. During the 2000 Sydney Olympics, superstars such as Ian Thorpe appeared on stamps overnight after winning gold. But it is not always a comfortable feeling, seeing your face peering back at you from the front of an envelope, as the champion swimmer revealed in a 2008 interview.

A few too many times I received fan mail with my stamp on it and it's really weird. If you send a fan letter with the stamp . . . it's almost bordering on that kind of stalker, crazy area . . . looking back at me it was a little off-putting . . . It's something that I think I'll be more astonished with as I get older and as all of these moments fade into memories [I'll think] this is a really good thing for me and part of my history to be able to show my family.

Australia Post's generosity of spirit did not go unnoticed when in 2004, Dame Joan Sutherland was honoured in its Australian Legends series. The decision would have brought to the minds of many Australia Post employees an earlier uproar generated by the diva, after a postal clerk requested she provide some identification.

Fondly reminiscing on the old days when Australians still carried British passports, the 67-year-old Dame Joan, a resident of Switzerland, complained to guests at a pro-monarchy lunch in Sydney in October 1994: 'When I go to the post office to be interviewed by a Chinese or an Indian—I'm not particularly racist—but I find it ludicrous, when I've had a passport for 40 years.' Dame Joan's off-the-cuff comments drew widespread brickbats from multiple corners. The president of the Australian Chinese Community Association, Lawrence Lau, said he was 'shell-shocked' by the remarks, while a representative of the Indian-Australian community, Dr Siddalingeswara Orekondy, denounced Dame Joan's comments as 'offensive and racist' and unworthy of her. 'Good singers should open their mouths to sing, and engage their brains before speaking,' suggested one letter to the *Sydney Morning Herald*.

An uncharacteristically tactful Prime Minister suggested the opera singer may have lived abroad a little too long. 'It's a long time since Dame Joan has been a part of the contemporary Australian political debate, if ever,' Paul Keating mused. 'I don't want her in this stage of her very distinguished and truly illustrious career caught up in a political debate which she really isn't familiar with.'

It was left up to the chairman of the Australian Republican Movement, Malcolm Turnbull, to point out the irony of an

Australian choosing 'to live in a republic, Switzerland, while lecturing Australians not to choose a similar option'.

Over the past century and a half, the stamp has become more than a payment for a service. It has become a work of art—and as such, appropriately controversial at times—to be collected, forged, traded and stolen. That little piece of perforated paper has mirrored Australian history and promoted a young nation to a world that was only just beginning to get to know her.

CHAPTER 10

PHILATELIC FIXATIONS

A stamp is a little ambassador for Australia. Next to the country's flag, it's very, very important.
RAY CHAPMAN

As soon as the Penny Black was issued, the first stamp collector was born. Now there are millions of philatelists, amateur and professional, across the world, trading in millions of dollars worth of objects every year. Ray Chapman is one of Australia's most renowned philatelists and today his treasured collection is housed in the Post Master Gallery in Melbourne. But Chapman's decision to sell his collection to Australia Post in 1986 was not without controversy, nor violence.

'I was very keen for Australia Post to have the collection and they had shown their interest and they rang and asked me what I wanted for it,' Chapman recalls, 'and I thought, well, $750,000 because over 40 years I think I would have spent probably six to seven hundred thousand on it. I couldn't afford to give it but I was very proud to think they thought it was good enough to put in their Post Master Gallery.'

By handing the collection over to Australia Post, Chapman's 40-year passion could be shared by an entire nation. But to the serious stamp collector, Chapman's decision meant the coveted rarities he had spent a lifetime gathering would never come on the market again.

'That meant all the rarities in the Ray Chapman collection were effectively locked up and outside of the potential ownership of future generations of stamp collectors,' says stamp dealer Glen Stephens. 'And this didn't play down well with the serious collectors of the time who take the view as most collectors do that all collectors are just temporary custodians of whatever they own.'

Chapman reckons the collection he sold to Australia Post more than 20 years ago is probably worth about $10 million today. Stephens believes it's closer to $15 million '. . . and it's all in the hands of the Post Office so it won't be coming back on the market,' he says. '[It] is an unfortunate turn of events for stamp collectors of the future.'

To pay for the Chapman Collection and establish itself in the future buyers' market, Australia Post moved to auction off a $1 million portion of its archived stamps, thought to be worth well over $10 million in total. It was a decision which polarised the philatelic community, with some collectors and dealers predicting that an artificially generated glut of stamps not previously sold over the post office counter would devalue the market as a whole. Others were less alarmed, arguing that the market could in fact be stimulated by the interest generated by Australia Post's sale. The *Sydney Morning*

Herald sided with the second group, arguing in January 1987: 'Suggestions that the sale will be a major dampener for the stamp market appear exaggerated. Several dealers put more through their own sales in a year than the total offering by Australia Post.'

Australia Post invited seven prominent stamp auction houses to prepare submissions, including information on their marketing strategies and commission rates. When Melbourne stamp auctioneer Charles Leski won the tender he saw it as the career opportunity of a lifetime. 'Initially I was very proud. To be known as Australia Post's official auctioneer was tremendous publicity, and I knew it would generate a lot of additional business,' he recalls. Then the death threats started.

Leski was aware of some rival auctioneers who, while publicly fanning the flames of outrage over Australia Post's decision to sell part of its archival stock and threatening to boycott the auction, had privately written to the organisation complaining about their lack of involvement. It was, as Leski said, an unparalleled opportunity for any Australian stamp auctioneer. He was offered unprecedented access to Australia Post's archived material, and effectively given carte blanche. From the millions of dollars worth of stock, he was required to select just enough material of his choosing to generate about $1 million in revenue for Australia Post. With his extensive philatelic experience and background in law and economics, Leski was confident he could curate a collection for auction without causing a crisis of confidence in the stamp market. As Leski finished making his selections and entered the preparation stage for the auction, the letters began arriving.

'There's one in particular I remember,' he recalls. 'The words were made from newspaper cuttings and the message read "bloody Jew, stop the auction or we'll kill you".' When the anonymous phone calls began, with the callers warning Leski they knew where his children went to school, the distraught auctioneer contacted the police. They assured him such threats were more common than people might think, and were almost always never carried through.

On the evening of 18 August 1986, Leski locked his office and walked alone to his car. At Melbourne's Malvern Town Hall, a throng of dealers and collectors were gathering for a major stamp auction Leski was to hold that night. As he went to unlock his car, the keys were suddenly wrenched from his hands. He was confronted by two men wearing balaclavas. He recalled being punched and kicked to the ground, all the while being subjected to an anti-Semitic tirade. 'I still really don't know if I was beaten up because I was Jewish, or because I had been chosen [by Australia Post]—or both,' he says. Clearly robbery had not been the purpose of the assault. Leski's car was stuffed with valuable stock for that evening's auction, and the vehicle was left untouched. Out of sheer anger and determination, Leski proceeded to that evening's auction. 'I thought if whoever had [ordered] this was in that room, I wanted to show them they hadn't won,' he says. Attending hospital later that night, he was treated for two fractured bones to his left hand.

Leski called a family meeting, including his elderly parents who, as Holocaust survivors, were devastated by their son's ordeal. The family agreed he should not proceed with the Australia Post auction. 'It was an easy decision, but one I was disappointed I had to make,' Leski says.

An agreement was reached for Leski to withdraw from the contract, and Australia Post announced it would sell the stamps by public tender instead. The archival sell-off would be a one-off event, Australia Post added. What appeared to have begun as a straightforward revenue-raising exercise to secure the Chapman Collection had turned into a personal and publicity disaster.

The subsequent sale was enormously successful, however, generating well in excess of the million-dollar target. And the bottom didn't fall out of the Australian philatelic market. Leski says he can't help a wry smile every time he reads a stamp's provenance proudly proclaiming its Australia Post archive sale origins. 'There's a lot of gold medal collections out there today that wouldn't exist, if it wasn't for that Australia Post sale,' he says.

Leski's assailants were never caught. 'It's still an open wound. And from time to time I wonder if I've since had a drink or shared a meal with the person who paid [those men].'

Two decades later, an Australian collection to rival Chapman's came on the market. Arthur Gray made a fortune from his Russell's chain of health food stores, and in 2001 he sold the business for a reputed $10 million. When he put his collection of classic Australian stamps on the market in 2006, it was predicted he would reap another $10 million.

Gray had been collecting stamps since the age of eight, and had an impressive cache of 'Roos'—Charles Frazer's kangaroo and map stamps which are so highly prized by philatelists throughout the world today. He told the *Australian Financial Review* he was selling the collection because it was complete, he had exhibited it as widely as he could, and had won as many medals as was possible.

In February 2006, the most valuable single catalogued offering of Australian stamps was transported to Shreve Philatelic Galleries in New York. So keen was the international interest in rare Roos and subsequent George V heads, the country they were to be auctioned in was irrelevant, Gray said. 'The stamps would sell as well if they were offered in a New York auction room or a tin shed in Coonabarabran— provided the shed had internet and phone connections,' he told the *AFR*.

Answering the critics who raised concerns the valuable stamps would be forever lost offshore, Gray pointed out that the Chapman Collection, safe in the hands of Australia Post, meant a complete set of Roos was assured permanent residency in Australia.

In February 2007, the New York auction of the Arthur Gray Collection fetched almost $7.2 million, including buyer's commission. It was the highest result for any single-issue stamp collection ever auctioned, and set a number of price records. It is believed many of the valuable stamps then made their way back to Australia, joining a number of private collections. Later that year, a set of four £1 brown and blue kangaroos fetched $265,395 at a Prestige Philately auction in Melbourne, while a 1913 £2 black and red kangaroo fetched $196,930.

※

Where there is money, inevitably there is crime. Forgeries are not uncommon in the stamp world, but their worth largely depends on who did the forging. In 2004, Prestige Philately knowingly sold a forged 1913 £2 kangaroo for more than $4000—and the auction house wasn't breaking any laws.

The fake stamp was the work of Jean de Sperati, forger extraordinaire (or, as Chapman prefers to put it, 'a bloody good forger'). The Italian-born French resident de Sperati only ever forged that one Australian stamp, and whenever such a rarity comes on the market, thousands of dollars change hands.

An industrial chemist by trade, de Sperati had a vocation; the money he made from his expertly crafted fakes was merely incidental to the enjoyment he gained from the duplicity, and the challenge of improving on the post office's original. Such was his talent in accurately reproducing valuable stamps, he earned the title 'the Rubens of Philately'.

De Sperati began his experimentations in forgery in the 1920s, reproducing valuable stamps from San Marino. The fakes fooled the experts, and the delight this gave him spurred on the bored chemist to branch out. He would eventually produce what is thought to be about 5000 master-quality forgeries of stamps from more than 100 different countries. De Sperati got away with it because he always signed his fakes very lightly on the back. Had his stamps been used as postage, it would have been a crime to send them across international borders.

This did not stop de Sperati from run-ins with the law, however. In 1942, a package posted to Portugal by de Sperati was intercepted by a French customs officer who smelt a rat. Despite de Sperati declaring on the outside of the package the contents were 'art reproductions of postage stamps' to the value of about 60,000 francs, the contents were handed over to philatelic experts for analysis. Much to de Sperati's amusement, no doubt, the experts examined the stamps and declared them genuine. De Sperati was charged by Vichy authorities with attempting to evade customs duties on rare goods valued at almost 300,000 francs.

The trial turned into a farce. De Sperati defended himself by arguing he had not broken any laws by sending his fully declared 'philatelic art' through the mail. The prosecution's case rested on the evidence of the philatelic experts who swore the de Sperati counterfeits were genuine. According to the philatelic network Stampez—a goldmine of much stamp trivia—during the course of the trial some of the genuine stamps got mixed up with the de Sperati forgeries, confounding everyone. The judge had to request the defendant to re-sort the evidence, as it appeared he was the only one capable of doing so.

As a last resort, de Sperati tendered to the court as evidence the tools of his trade, including sheets of old paper identical to those used to produce the valuable genuine stamps, along with his blocks and inks. This got him off the charge of attempting to evade customs, but failed to get him out of trouble. De Sperati was subsequently put on trial for forgery.

De Sperati's protestations that his all-consuming hobby was by no means underpinned by an intention to defraud for financial gain fell on deaf ears. He was convicted on a charge of criminal intention and sentenced to one year in prison. On the grounds of advanced age—he was already in his mid-60s at the time of his conviction—he was spared prison, but his forgery days were over. In 1954, de Sperati sold his entire stock of counterfeit stamps and equipment to the British Philatelic Association for more than 10 million francs. The sale not only provided the Italian with a comfortable nest egg for retirement, it also ensured that the forging equipment would not fall into the hands of another aspiring de Sperati. Three years later, at the age of 73, the Rubens of Philately died at his home in Aix-les-Bains, having stayed true to his word never to forge another stamp again.

Stories of stamp crime are by no means restricted to a bygone era, and Australia has a few contemporary stamp scandals of its own. In 2004, Sydney crime journalist Stephen Gibbs, reporting on what appeared to be a common larceny trial, uncovered a fascinating tale revolving around a police inspector, a judge, a valuable collection of stamps and a fortunate coincidence.

According to criminal folklore, Gibbs wrote in the *Sydney Morning Herald* in September 2004, notorious thug Chris Flannery had, some 20 years earlier, paid a visit to Sydney drug squad detective Mick Drury, as the officer lay fighting for his life in a Royal North Shore Hospital bed. Flannery had earlier attempted to assassinate the officer by firing two shots through his Chatswood kitchen window. In a scene worthy of Mario Puzo treatment, the hitman arrived at the hospital to finish off the job. Legend has it Flannery turned on his heels when he reached the ward, swarming as it was with blue uniforms. Only half the police were guarding their colleague Detective Drury, however. In a nearby bed lay Justice Raymond Watson, one of the victims of a series of bombings in the early 1980s related to the Family Court. Justice Watson had been seriously injured in the 1984 blast, which had killed his wife Pearl when she opened the door of the couple's Greenwich unit.

Drury and Watson had little in common other than a shared ward, unrequited justice (neither of their attackers was ever brought to justice; Flannery was believed to have been murdered about a year later, although his body was never found) and a love of stamps. Gibbs wrote:

> Twenty years later, Mick Drury, now a State Government adviser and world-recognised stamp expert, is sitting in Gabriele's Philatelic Service in Bridge Street, Sydney, when a man and woman approach the counter. Unknown to Drury, the woman is a carer for Ray Watson, now an invalid in a retirement home. She is carrying part of a $50,000 stamp collection the judge has assembled in a lifetime's collecting.
>
> To the former detective and stamp expert, the conversation between the woman, known in subsequent court action as WS, and Gabriele's employee Damien Maurice did not seem right. The retired inspector, who has collected stamps for at least 40 of his 50 years and is vice-president of the Australian Commonwealth Collectors Club of NSW, became increasingly suspicious. The woman appeared to have no idea of the value of the stamps, or any personal affinity with the collection. He did not believe they belonged to her.

According to evidence heard in court, the woman refused a $2000 cheque offered that day by Maurice for two of the stamps—a £1 kangaroo and a £2 kangaroo. Instead she promised she would return with more. Less than a month later, the Bridge Street store received another visit, this time from Justice Watson's daughter, Rose Parkin. Handing over the judge's stamp collection for dealer Gabriele Woodbine to inspect, it was found that a large section of the collection was missing. Based on what Drury had witnessed at the dealer's a month earlier, the connection was made between the mysterious woman in possession of the valuable Roos and the judge's decimated collection.

Having suffered a stroke a year earlier, Watson was being cared for by WS in a nursing home serviced apartment. It was while he was hospitalised for a fall, the court heard, that the stamps went missing. Stamps were the 81-year-old judge's most prized possessions, Gibbs wrote.

> He had thousands of stamps, the most valuable from early Australia, Great Britain and America, kept locked in a cabinet at the nursing home, the key around his wrist. Each year, with the arrival of a new Stanley Gibbons catalogue, the encyclopaedia of philately, the judge would sit at his desk and mark off each stamp he owned.

The stamps were returned, but no conviction against the judge's carer was recorded. Due to Watson's mental frailty, the prosecutor was unable to prove the judge had not given the stamps to his carer as a gift, as WS had claimed. While the magistrate hearing the case described WS's defence as 'somewhat dubious' and that given the judge's incapacity it was 'grossly inappropriate' for WS to have accepted them anyway, the magistrate agreed that there was insufficient proof for conviction.

Better known to most Australians is the story of a fatally flawed premier, his passion for rare stamps and the part they played in his ultimate downfall. Former Western Australian Premier Brian Burke found himself behind bars for the second time in 1997 after being convicted of misappropriating more than $122,000 from his own party. The politician turned

Ambassador to Ireland and the Holy See and now political lobbyist, whose name still spells trouble for any Federal Labor politician caught breaking bread with him, had dreams in the mid-1980s of establishing a 'Burke Collection' of early Australian stamps. Burke claimed he intended to present the collection as an investment to the Australian Labor Party at a later date, which explains why he allegedly used money in a party donation account he controlled to purchase the stamps. In the fallout of the WA Inc inquiry, the justice system thought otherwise. Burke served just five months of his three-year sentence, however, before his convictions were quashed. He walked free after a Court of Appeal found there was insufficient evidence to prove the funds used by Burke to purchase the stamps did in fact belong to the ALP.

The judge, the detective and the disgraced politician are in colourful company. Among the 20th- and 21st-century figures known for their passion for rare stamps are Field Marshal Erwin Rommel and former aide to George W. Bush, Karl Rove. Other prominent American politicians famous for their collecting habits included Dwight D. Eisenhower and Franklin D. Roosevelt. Queen Elizabeth II inherited her grandfather George V's obsession, while other notable royals with philatelic leanings include Prince Rainier of Monaco and King Carol II of Romania, who escaped into exile in 1940 with a stamp collection thought to be one of the most valuable in the world at that time.

In a celebrity-soaked world, sometimes a collection's worth has more to do with who did the collecting rather than the intrinsic value of the stamps involved. After Freddie Mercury, lead singer of the rock band Queen, died in 1991, his boyhood stamp album was purchased by the British Postal Service for almost $A5000, and is now on display at the National Postage Museum. John Lennon's childhood stamp album did even better. According to stamp dealer Glen Stephens, Lennon's collection was 'dirty, dog-eared, creased and stained' and contained no more than a couple of hundred near-worthless stamps. The Smithsonian National Postal Museum in Washington DC nevertheless bought the album for more than $A73,000 in 2005.

Australia's avid top-end collectors might look a little stolid in comparison. Along with Arthur Gray, Hugh Morgan, former chief executive of Western Mining, is considered one of the country's most prolific philatelists. It is widely believed that in 2006 Morgan paid $225,875 at auction for two unaccepted designs entered in that first Common-wealth stamp design competition back in the early 1900s, from which the Roo emerged victorious. And while only some might be prepared to confer on New Zealander Sir Ron Brierley honorary Australian status, the corporate raider with numerous Australian interests is a forceful player in collecting circles.

According to Stephens, it is not unknown for Brierley to complete transactions of a million dollars at a time, and a 'messy lot' gives him a great thrill—he loves a good challenge. After Gray's kangaroos went to auction in New York in 2006, Brierley's explanation as to why he took no interest in the bidding, was, according to Stephens, because 'all the work was already done . . . there was no fun for me in that sort of collection'.

✖

Be they erudite or eccentric, veteran or virgin, the hundreds of thousands of collectors have been embraced by Australia Post over the past quarter of a century, providing a huge range of products and information on its websites, in its magazines, bulletins and public exhibitions, and at philatelic counters across the country. But this has not necessarily always been the case. Fastidious philatelists were not particularly popular in the PMG's Department when the decision was made to create the position of Philatelic Officer in 1951. Phil Collas, a former editor of *Australian Stamp Monthly*, nonetheless set about establishing a professional philatelic service. Within two years Collas had set up philatelic bureaux for counter and mail-order sales at all GPOs, and had launched the first edition of the *Philatelic Bulletin*—which later was to become the *Australian Stamp Bulletin*—to inform collectors of stamps and postmarks about to be released.

Postal historian and Australia Post curator Richard Breckon says the new philatelic bureaux were enormously useful to stamp dealers, whose relationship with the Post Office had not always been cosy. Writing for the Australasian Philatelic Traders Association (APTA), Breckon recalls an October 1949 meeting of the Australasian Stamp Dealers Association (a precursor to the APTA) where dealers' patience had reached the limit over what they saw as sloppy work from postal employees. Much of a rare stamp's worth has always relied on the hand stamp being well-centred and applied evenly enough to ensure the item's date and place of postage are legible. A spate of bad centring, the association believed, was due to 'poor quality girl labour who were careless in their handling of the sheets' at the Note Printing Branch.

Following Collas's appointment, the stamp dealers were assured the philatelic bureaux would not be competitors but provide 'the best possible service to dealers and collectors', according to Breckon. As Philatelic Officer, part of Collas's job was to serve as Secretary to the Stamp Advisory Committee, which continues to play an important advisory role to Australia Post's Philatelic Group today. Comprised of artists, designers, philatelists and community figures, the committee advises on such matters as choice of artist and subject matter for new stamps, as well as considering requests for new stamps from community groups and organisations. Two years of advance planning and one year of development goes into the creation of a new stamp, with the committee formulating and overseeing the design brief.

Collas played a hands-on role in the production and design of Australian stamps in the 17 years he served as inaugural Philatelic Officer, and he did not shy away from political decisions. It was he who released the world's first Christmas stamps, as counter-propaganda in the Cold War climate of the 1950s; atheism was commonly associated with communism. The first Australian Antarctic Territory stamps were also issued in 1957 under Collas, followed by those of the Cocos (Keeling) Islands in 1963. Collas was a fervent believer that one of a country's most effective means of establishing sovereignty over questionable territory could be achieved through the issue of distinctive stamps. Under Collas, the mammoth task of making the transition to decimal currency was also completed, and by the time he retired in 1969, the Post Office's previously chaotic philatelic collection had been thoroughly sorted and archived.

Philately has changed dramatically since Collas's time. Today, international networks for buying, selling and trading jostle for space on the internet, connecting collectors from Hobart to Helsinki. Contemporary philatelists pale at the very idea of steaming stamps off brown paper packages and envelopes, let alone disturbing the gum of a stamp by attaching a hinge. The market has broadened, from stamps alone to the envelopes and packaging (covers) themselves, providing the myriad stamps, tags and labels are extant. A large part of the thrill of postal history is deciphering the stamps, stickers and franking, and piecing together the story behind the package. The growing popularity of postal history enabled veteran enthusiast Max Watson to sell his collection of covers titled 'Registered Mail of Victoria 1840–1912' for more than $200,000 in 2005. The same year, a post-World War II Myer Emporium food parcel label, rare purely because so few were ever kept, was valued at $2000.

Reporting on a Prestige Philately auction in 2005, the *Sydney Morning Herald*'s James Cockington found that a 1961 Qantas aerogramme was valued at $200 purely because it was addressed in Chinese, while a 1906 registered letter sent from Hobart was valued at $1000 solely on the grounds of size—the standard-issue envelopes sold in Hobart's post offices at that time were known to be the smallest in the British Empire. Despite never being sent, a 1916 cover used for sending wool samples to England was valued at $3000. No used examples of these envelopes have ever emerged, perhaps not surprisingly, given that fewer than 2000 were ever printed. Some of the most highly prized items today had the capacity to destroy lives in their time. After the dreaded knock from the telegram boy, a package—known as a 'deceased kit'—would inevitably follow, weeks or months later, bearing the label 'this article which has been accepted at packet-rate of postage by authority of the Postmaster-General must not be opened whilst in the custody of the Department but must be delivered in the present Sealed condition'. The paper wrapping the possessions of soldiers killed in World War I can now fetch more than $3000 each.

※

Unquantifiable billions of items have been processed by Australian postal services since 1809. Inevitably, many thousands of letters and parcels, most lovingly sent, were never to reach their destination. The vaguely addressed, the illegible, and the incomprehensible would invariably end up at the dead letter office. In 1970, a young writer and director called Fred Schepisi was called on by the Post Office to educate businesses on the importance of training their staff in the correct processing of mail, to avoid it going astray. Schepisi's corporate film, *Onward Speed*, is a light-hearted and informative piece of celluloid history, now housed in the National Archives of Australia. It features sibling actors Jon Finlayson and Rhonda Finlayson, with the latter also producing the film and later marrying its director. The background to the commissioning of the film, given by curator Adrienne Parr, reveals just how labour-intensive mailrooms were before the days of electronic post:

> The film, directed at executives, secretaries and mail room staff, humorously instructs its audience in the efficient

management of business mail. In the days before computers, everything was documented on paper and everything was posted by snail mail. Multiple carbon copies were made of every letter typed. These copies, along with correspondence received, were placed in paper files and passed back and forth between individuals within the organisation. The competent collection and delivery of all this paper was critical, and the mail rooms of large office buildings and big business organisations were major affairs.

It seems like Australians are still learning how to address their mail correctly. Each year Australia Post auctions off thousands of undeliverable items. The 2007 lot consisting of some 15,000 items included a wedding dress, a Louis Vuitton designer handbag with matching saxophone case, a sitar, two guitars, 27 coffee machines and 400 bottles of wine. And that was in Victoria alone.

The rise of internet shopping in recent years has only added to the pile of homeless mail. In January 2008, *The Age* reported an explosion in the number of illegal items being posted to Australia. In the preceding 12 months, 100,000 prohibited items had been seized either by the Australian Quarantine and Inspection Service (AQIS) or intercepted by Australia Post inspectors. Banned items included live honey bees, baby snakes concealed in video cassette boxes, exotic bulbs and seeds, cheeses, fruits, meat, eggs, and even insects highly prized by Chinese herbalists. A woman had even posted some of her cat's fur to a friend in Australia 'who liked to knit with unusual materials', while a leg of ham dispatched from France included a note from the sender boasting how he had hidden the meat in soap 'to fool the sniffer dogs'. AQIS warned that the flood of foreign-bought foodstuffs and other items into Australia could lead to a 'potentially devastating breach of the biosecurity safeguards'. *The Age* noted that in 2001 only 5 per cent of foreign parcels were being X-rayed. By 2007, all overseas packages were undergoing scanning.

'The biggest growth area for us is in items ordered from foreign websites,' AQIS's spokesman, Carson Creagh, complained. 'The websites themselves do not know the rules in Australia so they are just sending this stuff out . . . they may not even care because they have already got their money so it's the customer who loses out.'

One of the most macabre and absurd postal items ever to arrive on Australian shores is probably the urn containing the ashes of a beloved deceased. The parcel from Britain was accompanied by a note: 'Here's Harry, he always wanted to visit Australia.'

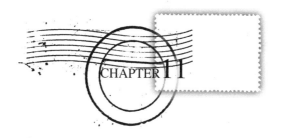

CHALLENGES OF THE
ELECTRONIC AGE

Today over 20 million articles are handled by Australia Post each day. But has mail become an endangered species? Among generations X and Y, the art of letter writing—'snail mail'—is already regarded as an archaic pursuit. With the proliferation of e-mail, the internet and mobile phones, does each click of the mouse or beep of an SMS signal the looming death of traditional postal services?

Bernard Salt, a cultural and demographic commentator with KPMG, says there is no denying we don't write as many personal letters as we once did. To receive a personal letter can be quite an occasion in a household—an announcement of sorts, or a sign that something's gone wrong. But even today, it would be inconceivable to receive such a thing as a wedding invitation, or a message of condolence, by e-mail or text message.

In reality, the rapid rise of new technologies has not decreased the day-to-day volume of mail handled by Australia Post, but merely changed its nature. It is estimated that mobile phone bills account for an extra five million letters going through the system each month, and the parcel delivery business is booming as more people embrace the convenience of mail-order catalogues and shopping online through the internet.

The ability to cater for massive volumes of bulk mail was a skill Australia Post developed more than three decades ago, with the introduction of a new bulk local rate for large lodgements of mail and reduced charges for 'to the householder' addressed mail. By 1978, some 3400 bulk direct-mail campaigns had combined to put an extra one million articles through the mail. Bulk direct-mail services, offering substantial discounts, succeeded in making the post a more attractive option for advertisers, and as signs of 'no junk mail' and 'Australia Post only' become a more common sight on Australian letter boxes today, the popularity of householder-addressed mail among businesses has not abated.

Improvements in the speed and efficiency of mail processing occurred steadily through the 1980s. New indexing desks and letter-sorting machines installed in metropolitan mail centres from 1985 enabled postal officers to index or key-in a postcode, which then appeared on the envelope as a machine-readable barcode. The barcoded mail was then fed through sorting machines which had the capacity to process around 30,000 letters an hour.

But there was also the constant question of deregulation, and government concerns over issues of competition and monopolies. A public inquiry into the statutory functions and duties of the Australian Postal Commission was launched in September 1981. A year later, the inquiry's chairman, A.E. Bradley, recommended Australia Post's monopoly should be retained, but that its door-to-door courier service was anti-competitive and should be dismantled. The ban proved short-lived, however, with the government giving the green light for Australia Post's re-entry into the courier business three years later.

It had been within its courier services that Australia Post, in partnership with Telecom Australia, had begun the first foray into electronic post as early as 1977. 'One day the handwritten or typed letter will be transmitted over the telephone network,' former Australian Post Office Director-General Trevor Housely predicted back in 1968. It had taken less than a decade for that prediction to become reality. From the late 1970s, the march towards the computer age inevitably raised questions about the place of traditional mail in an uncertain new world of electronic communications. The arrival of the facsimile escalated the debate considerably. It was, of course, the logical electronic extension of the century-old telegraph. But would mail volumes plummet as this extraordinary new invention, capable of sending images as well as text through a telephone cable, took hold?

In 1984, little more than seven years from its earliest experiments, Australia Post launched its public facsimile service, Intelpost. Promoted as 'the fastest mail on earth', the capacity for two-hour local deliveries within Australia and next working-day delivery for overseas destinations, made Intelpost an instant hit with businesses. Initial sales exceeded forecasts by 125 per cent, and within four years a network of fax machines linked over 500 post offices throughout the country. Australia's first facsimile service would later be re-badged FaxPost, but at the time, the term facsimile, let alone its abbreviation 'fax', might as well have been a foreign word. 'We felt the word facsimile would not be understood by the public, so we used a name which was more common in other parts of the world,' recalls Dr David Smyth, who headed the Electronic Postal Service Department at the time. On the occasion of Australia's bicentennial celebrations, the enormous strides achieved in written communication over two centuries was no more evident than when the tall ship HMAV *Bounty* swept through Sydney Heads under full sail, bearing the giant Australia Post logo and the brand Intelpost on its topsail.

A year after Intelpost's launch, the world's first commercial electronic mail service by a postal administration was launched in Australia. Businesses could now lodge messages with E-Post, via telephone, telex or over the counter for high-speed transmissions. The lettergram also went online in 1985, enabling businesses to send bulk mail-outs electronically. A single copy of the text and a list of all its intended recipients was all that was needed for mass delivery within a two-hour time frame. Operators simply keyed in the information, which was then relayed electronically to the print facility closest to each recipient's address. The text was then printed out, placed in an envelope and delivered. The Imagegram service commenced soon after. The service launched with Sydney GPO sending a sketch of the Opera House and Harbour Bridge to Melbourne's GPO, and Melbourne responding with an image of St Kilda Road's Arts Centre spire. By the early 1990s, electronic counter terminals were making their way into all the major metropolitan post offices. Successful trials in Victoria and then Tasmania had seen business quadruple in many of the piloted program's outlets and paved the way for a roll-out of an electronic point-of-sale system across the nation.

※

By the time the Hawke Government announced in 1988 that Australia Post's government strings were to be severed, such was the institution's complex combination of statutory obligation and business enterprise, the move to corporatisation was seen as an opportunity to embrace the freedoms of adulthood. Only one thing stood in Australia Post's way.

The relationship between the institution and its work-force had become increasingly toxic throughout the 1980s. Organisational stability had been rocked by escalating industrial strife and bitter stand-offs, crippling relations between management, staff and unions. At the core of the animosity was the frightening pace of change. The very real threat of job losses forced unions to dig in their heels, while executives knew that to ignore progress would be tantamount to corporate suicide. The endless cycle of stop-works, Industrial Tribunal mediation and the subsequent trade-offs of higher wages for staff cooperation was clearly only treating the symptoms, and not the cause of the malaise. Staff still felt disenfranchised and baulked at each new measure of efficiency and progress.

Industrial unrest had plagued the $6 million Redfern Mail Exchange in Sydney since its opening in 1965. As the

Fraser Government's Minister for Communications, Tony Staley, put it, the 1980s would culminate in 'a number of almighty stoushes'.

Hailed as the largest mechanised mail centre and the most advanced facility of its kind in the Southern Hemisphere, the mail exchange at its peak employed some 3600 staff in a 24-hour-a-day, seven-days-a-week operation. The harbinger of high-technology mail handling, the New South Wales plant was the first of what had planned to be a roll-out of automated centralised sorting centres across every state. Within just a few years, however, the PMG's Department was grappling with continual arbitration and staff dissatisfaction from a massive, strongly unionised workforce, forcing the department to create its own Industrial Relations Division. By 1972, it had become clear that the centralisation experiment was failing abysmally. Redfern recorded a 10 per cent fall in productivity, while in Melbourne, which had had its own centralised mail exchange placed on hold, productivity *increased* by 13 per cent. But despite the frequent stoppages which threatened to halt mail delivery in New South Wales, the PMG was reluctant to abandon its $6 million investment. The workplace unrest continued unabated throughout the 1970s, and it took a crippling two-week strike in late 1985 for Australia Post to finally decommission the country's largest mail exchange. The mail sorting process was once more divested to suburban and regional exchanges and the Redfern site marked for redevelopment, eventually becoming Australian Post's New South Wales headquarters.

In 1988, Victoria's Clayton South Mail Centre appeared to hold the key to resolving Australia Post's industrial relations problems. The centre was responsible for almost half of Melbourne's metropolitan mail, and a series of well-coordinated work bans had succeeded in practically bringing services to a halt. By this time, the Industrial Relations Commission was fed up. In early 1989, Commissioner John Lewin decided to investigate matters for himself and convened a series of meetings between union representatives and management. He engaged independent facilitator Tony Briscomb, head of the Royal Melbourne Institute of Technology's Industrial Participation Unit, to chair the sessions and, after protracted and often vitriolic confrontations, the ultimate result was a signed Joint Statement of Understanding on Industrial Participation between management and unions in 1989. Rather than engaging in pre-emptive industrial action, the unions agreed to allow local problems to be resolved through the appropriate channels. In return, management agreed not to implement radical change without appropriate consultation with its workforce. The success at Clayton South prompted Australia Post to embark on a national program of industrial participation training, a turning point which allowed the transition to corporatisation to go ahead with reasonable confidence.

Towards the close of a tumultuous decade, an unspoken emotional truce between management and staff quietly united a workforce struggling to come to terms with a devastating event. At 4 p.m. on 8 December 1987, Frank Vitkovic made his way to the State Office Building in Melbourne's Queen Street. Armed with a sawn-off M1 rifle, the law school drop-out was seeking revenge over an imagined slight by former schoolmate Con Margelis, who worked on the fifth floor in the Telecom Credit Union. After Margelis escaped, Vitkovic opened fire indiscriminately, killing 19-year-old Judith Morris instantly. Less than 15 minutes later, another seven Australia Post employees lay dead or dying, as Vitkovic carried out his killing spree among the plastic Christmas trees, tinsel and lemonade laid out for a staff Christmas party that afternoon. He made his way up to Australia Post's 12th-floor philatelic sales department, claiming the lives of 18-year-old Annunziata Avignone and 20-year-old Julie McBean. The body of David Spencer, 29, was later found slumped over the office photocopier. The killer moved down a floor to Australia Post's data-processing and finance departments. Michael McGuire, a father of three who had been expected home early that afternoon for his daughter's fifth birthday party, was shot at point-blank range. Rodney Brown lay dying at the desk he had worked at for the past seven years. Marianne Van Ewyk-Sharp and Catherine Dowling died clinging to each other as they crouched in terror under a desk.

Tony Gioia, Australia Post's assistant finance manager, brought the slaughter to an end, tackling the gunman to the ground. Finance clerk Frank Carmody, who had sustained wounds from four of the gunman's bullets, wrestled the rifle from Vitkovic's hands. Neither man could hold the killer down long enough to prevent him reaching a window and plunging to his death 11 floors below.

Gioia and Carmody received Australia's second-highest bravery decoration, the Star of Courage, for their actions that day. Australia Post set up a fund to assist the victims' families. It was Australia's largest mass killing at the time, and remains Victoria's worst.

※

On 1 July 1989, Australia Post became a corporate entity. But along with the right of independence, corporatisation demanded the responsibility of profit, delivered to its sole shareholder, the Commonwealth. In addition, the newly corporatised Australia Post was required to pay state and local government taxes, federal excise duty and corporate income tax. As its future chairwoman, Linda Nicholls, remarked at the time: 'We had to stop acting like a government department and start acting like a real business.'

Corporatisation did not, however, absolve Australia Post from the responsibility of its community service obligations to maintain accessible and affordable mail delivery for all Australians. Accordingly, the government initially agreed to reserve the carriage of all domestic and international mail up to 500 grams exclusively for Australia Post. The remainder of its business, however, was open to competition.

At the time of corporatisation, Australia Post owned the largest network of any retailer in the country, yet its operations were sustaining $100-million-a-year losses. Many of the 4400 post offices nationwide had been built more than 100 years ago and were ill equipped to house the multiple layers of new technology which had accumulated over recent decades. Moreover, the rise of the shopping mall meant that post offices traditionally located in the main streets of many suburbs and towns were no longer at the hub of retail activity. Yet the obligation to maintain service delivery and access did not allow the corporation the luxury of cutting its operating costs by closing unprofitable branches. At the 1988 Brisbane World Expo, Australia Post successfully trialled a new-generation post office tailored to meet modern retail requirements. The

PostShop was born, and by 1991, Australia Post was snapping up retail premises around the country and converting them to one-stop postal shops. This innovation effectively removed the 'office' from the post office. The commercially unviable dual function which had been in operation for almost two centuries was split. Front-counter sales and service became the business of the PostShop, while the behind-the-scenes sorting of mail and delivery by posties became part of a massive relocation plan, in which these operations were shifted to purpose-built mail-sorting or delivery centres.

With the opening of the PostShops came a $70-million roll-out of EPOS (electronic point of sale) technology, enabling a wide range of bills to be paid in the one location. In 1995, EPOS bill payments and Commonwealth Bank transactions—which had been processed manually by the Post Office for almost 80 years—hit the 100 million mark, a 34 per cent increase over the previous year.

The PostShops also heralded the establishment of a single 6 p.m. deadline for mail. The uniform closing time was easier for customers to adhere to and streamlined delivery schedules. The 6 p.m. deadline also brought into being Express Post. Overnight delivery had previously been possible with the additional earlier afternoon deadline. Now another overnight service—without the premium price a courier service attracted—needed to be found. Australia Post launched Express Post on 1 October 1991, wooing the corporation's biggest business customers in Melbourne by posting an Express Post envelope containing the mastheads of Sydney's afternoon papers from the day before, and Melbourne's afternoon paper mastheads to its business clientele in Sydney. Express Post took off immediately, doubling its volume within a year.

Within two years of corporatisation, Australia Post's productivity was outpacing national growth, rising by 4.2 per cent during 1992. The same year, the price of the basic postal rate rose from 43 cents to 45 cents. The price hike came, however, with a pledge to in future lift productivity, not prices. The 45-cent rate remained frozen for the next 11 years, giving Australians the third-lowest postal rate in the Western world. In 1994, productivity increased by 6.8 per cent, and the Commonwealth Government received a $90-million after-tax dividend. Standard & Poor's subsequently awarded the corporation an AAA classification.

While the 1990s showed Australia Post was exceeding expectations in virtually all aspects of its corporatisation, it was also a decade in which the corporation was obliged to face four government reviews, in a bid to fully deregulate the postal services. Deregulation had been articulated in the Industry Commission's 1991 to 1993 review but rejected by the Keating Government. The corporation's monopoly was nevertheless diluted, lowering the cap from 500 grams to 250 grams for Australia Post's exclusive handling of inter-national and domestic mail. Two years later, a House of Representatives inquiry found that should deregulation go ahead, there was a distinct possibility that services to the bush and regional communities could be compromised.

In 1997, a third review, this time by the National Competition Council, resulted in the Howard Government lowering the cap to 50 grams for domestic letters, while removing all barriers to competition for the carriage of international mail. Given

a three-year time limit to phase in the changes, Australia
Post began moving into one of the most deregulated postal
markets in the world, with only New Zealand, Finland, Sweden
and Argentina operating with lower barriers. The corporation
pledged to the 29 per cent of Australians living in rural and
regional areas that no services to the bush would be cut. The
45-cent universal letter rate would remain, with urban areas
effectively subsidising mail deliveries in rural areas, where the
real cost could be anywhere up to $20 per letter.

At the same time, it became clear that despite the arrival
of the electronic age, mail volumes would not be shrinking. In
1995, La Trobe University research warned Australia Post to
expect a 35 to 40 per cent increase in deliveries over the next
decade—a predicted 22 million articles each day by 2005. The
now largely decentralised nature of mail sorting in the most
populated states gave managers little cause for optimism over
how the corporation might cope with such volumes.

Once again, the centralisation of mail sorting was thrust
back onto the agenda. With a détente of sorts established
between management and unions, economies of scale could
now be explored. Project FuturePost involved the construction
of two new centralised mail facilities in Dandenong in Melbourne and Strathfield in Sydney, at a cost of $99 million and
$169 million respectively. State-of-the-art letter-sorting equip-
ment was commissioned for the two biggest mail-sorting
centres ever built in Australia. Multi-lined optical character
readers had the capacity to stamp more than nine million
different barcodes. The technology worked by reading the
entire address of a letter, then placing a thin iridescent orange
line across the envelope.

Introduced in 1999, the barcoding technology was the centrepiece of the $500-million FuturePost project, and was the most revolutionary development in mail-handling in more than three decades. With a world standard postal network by the turn of the millennium, Australia Post's transformation had been, according to *Business Review Weekly*, 'one of the most remarkable in Australian corporate history', and the corporation was ushered into the league of Australia's top-40 companies.

DELIVERING TO A NATION

In the olden days the post office was made to look important because it really was important. It was partly that the post office thought itself important, but so did everyone else. It was a whole social thing. The post office was the centre of the town and distances were measured from post office to post office. Even in the small towns in Australia, if you had a post office, a church and a school, you had a town.

DR ELIZABETH FARRELLY, ARCHITECTURE CRITIC

From the outset of the building boom in the late 19th century, post offices set about making big statements, and they made them in stone. As the first colonial stamps were introduced from 1850 onwards, governments embarked on ambitious capital works programs to house their rapidly expanding postal services. The colony that was about to become known as Victoria already had over 30 post offices by 1849. But after the gold rush hit, post-office construction proliferated in all the colonies. The colonial governments saw that it was vital that each rural centre be serviced by its own post office, if only to serve as a symbol of civilisation. According to the Australian Heritage Council 'Government architects built enormous post offices in major provincial towns as statements of the authority and presence of the government'. 'These buildings were designed intentionally to make a statement that the Australian colonies were civilised British countries.'

This ideological underpinning meant the great Australian post offices of the 19th century looked remarkably different from their equivalents in the frontier towns of the United States at that time. The post office was not as central to the identity of the American wild west, because there was not the same need to assert a sense of British civilisation.

It was not unusual for town planners to incorporate the post office into a town's official precinct, which would typically include a police station, courthouse and sundry government administrative buildings. If possible, even a central railway station would be incorporated. As dual symbols of man's extra-ordinary progress and modernity, the architecture of both railway station and post office would compete on a scale of grandiosity. Not only did the post offices of colonial Australia become the marking points from town to town; with their imposing clock towers visible widely across the city, the GPOs became 'a clear symbol of the post office's role in regulating the pace of business and social interaction throughout each colony'.

Today, Sydney's GPO is a gourmand's paradise. The stables where the mail delivery horses were once fed and groomed is now a watering hole for well-heeled city business people, the dock master's office an up-market steakhouse, the sandstone-tunnelled mail sorting room a wine and cheese bar. Today's GPO reflects the obsessions and aspirations of contemporary Sydneysiders as much as it did 130 years ago.

Sydney's GPO was the Sydney Opera House of its day. Its construction, spread over three decades, came at enormous expense and was to polarise public opinion before gaining belated recognition. An 1862 government report into the postal department concluded that Sydney was in need of a new post office that would be the 'centre and focus, the heart . . . from which the pulse of civilisation throbs to the remotest extremity of the land'.

Controversially, official Colonial Architect James John-stone Barnet's subsequent design was conspicuously European, rather than English, to suit the Australian climate. And the building's sheer scale was initially criticised as unnecessary and extravagant. The ground floor housed mail receiving and sorting rooms, an electric telegraphy office, registry and money ordering offices, as well as private box facilities and posting windows. The mezzanine and first floors were to house the post office's administrative staff, laboratories and workshops, while the telegraph operating room was to take up most of the second floor. Staff facilities and storerooms were to be located on the third floor.

On 1 September 1874, thousands of Sydneysiders crowded the George Street pavement to witness the official opening ceremony, with the newly appointed Postmaster-General, Saul Samuel, declaring that the Sydney General Post Office 'will not be surpassed by any other similar structure in the Southern Hemisphere'. Marcella Hunter's history of Australian postal services describes newspaper reports of a dazzling day:

> The scene outside was most picturesque ... the interior
> was 'en regele' with fine examples of frescoing. Everything
> was in harmony, from the soft colours, wall stencilling and
> carpet design, to the ceiling decoration and rich hangings
> descending from massive gilt cornices over the windows.

The rapid rate of progress during the 1870s in the field of
postal and telegraphic services was such, however, that just a
few years after the GPO's opening the building was deemed
inadequate. In the 1880s, Barnet moved to the second phase
of construction, and by 1887 the GPO extended all the way
back to Pitt Street, occupying an entire city block. In 1882,
Barnet had engaged the services of sculptor Tommaso Sani to
decorate the Pitt Street facade and it was this decision which
would provoke almost a decade of vitriolic debate over the
building's artistic merits.

Commissioned for the sum of £800, Sani was briefed by
Barnet to glorify the arts, sciences and commerce of the
day by depicting contemporary Australians 'in realistic form'.
The result was to become known by its critics as 'Barnet's
Blot'. The carvings' completion in August 1883 was met with
abuse in Parliament and an outpouring of public opinion, with
letters to the Sydney papers describing the Sani sculptures
as 'grotesque and inartistic' and 'terrible travesties'. An
editorial in one newspaper described the carvings as 'repulsive
caricatures of contemporary life which grin and ogle from the
perch on the Post Office'.

Such was the government's concern over the apparent
affront to public taste, a board of inquiry was convened three
months after the carvings were unveiled. In defence of Sani's

work, Barnet argued that artistic realism was all the vogue in Europe at the time and that the sculptor's 'bold and dashing stroke of the chisel . . . shows the artist's power of producing a masterly effect of life and reality with a few touches'. The board of inquiry thought otherwise, concluding that while Barnet's intentions had been well-meaning, the carvings were 'far more to the unnatural and burlesque than . . . to the real' and their removal was ordered. A subsequent stay of execution was granted, however, after the Postmaster-General, James Norton, intervened on Barnet's behalf. By the time the GPO's extensions were nearing completion in 1886, such was the affection the Sani sculptures had earned in the intervening years, the Legislative Council was obliged to officially pronounce them bona fide works of art. An editorial in the *Daily Telegraph* on 20 March 1886, concluded that the newly completed Sydney GPO had encapsulated perfectly the city's identity:

Our successors, in the centuries to come, might readily see in this stately tower, rising from a building through which written words alive with human thoughts and feelings flow with a ceaseless and mighty current, and itself so closely linked with the lives of the people, a semi-conscious organism of the public life [rather] than a dead structure of irresponsive sandstone.

It was to be another five years, however, before the building was to receive its crowning glory. The completion in 1891 of a seven-storey clock tower, including bells, made the Sydney GPO the tallest structure in the city. Its completion was widely celebrated. A Sydney lawyer by the name of Robert Garran, who would go on to play an integral role in Federation as one of Edmund Barton's key organisers and lobbyists, marked the occasion with a poem:

Ring forth, ye bells, begin to chime;
Ring in the right, ring out the wrong;
We've waited patiently and long,
Ring, welcome bells, it's nearly time . . .

Ring night and day, with clarion clang;
Ring in the good; ring out the ill;
But don't, as some folk say you will,
Ring down the tower in which you hang.

For the next 40 years the clock would be dutifully wound every day by the same man, Henry Daly.

※

The fact that the colonial post offices were—with the exception of South Australia—under the control of a cabinet minister attests to the importance the public institutions played in the colonies' social and economic life. As rural settlements developed and spread across the country, it was largely at the discretion of the colonies' individual Postmasters-General as to which settlements would be endowed with a post office, and when. It followed therefore that, just as the post office became a town's lifeblood, the role of postmaster—or postmistress, as the case often surprisingly was in an era when women were otherwise denied public positions of authority—developed considerable gravitas in the community.

That may have been somewhat difficult for Postmaster Benjamin Baxter to have appreciated back in 1838. As the fifth Melbourne postmaster in just two years, Baxter endured pitiful remuneration and primitive working conditions before he too resigned. The last straw was having to be rescued, along with his family, by rowing boat from their home and post office after heavy rains caused the Yarra River to flood—an undignified experience. By the time the sixth postmaster had settled into the job, the post office had been moved to a sturdy brick building, on the site where the Melbourne GPO sits today, and the role of postmaster recognised with an annual salary of £300.

A century later, Baxter would have been astounded by the sheer sophistication of the Australian postal services. Post offices' mail sorting rooms throughout the country were undergoing massive changes. Sydney GPO became the first to introduce mechanical mail handling, with almost 100,000 metres of circuit wire connecting kilometres of conveyor belts. The building was processing some 400 million postal items a year, in addition to providing money order, telegram and telephone services. With mechanisation removing much of the mindless labour, an increasing number of employees, particularly in the large city GPOs, were in need of formal training to conduct the more sophisticated aspects of postal work.

The Postal Institute was established after World War I to train telegraph messengers and postal clerks in Victoria. Beginning its life as a lending library, the institute went on to offer training courses, and by 1920 over 1200 students were enrolled. That same year, Sydney's Postal Institute was opened, and by 1925, there were state-based training centres, including regional and country branches, in all six states. In 1945 the various state-based centres merged to form the Australian Postal Institute, employee training and education becoming the responsibility of the Postal Training School. Students were expected to learn all aspects of a postal clerk's work, including morse telegraphy, and many an ambitious teenage telegraph messenger would pass through the doors of the school in a bid to rise through the post office ranks.

Base grade entry to the public service via the post office was invariably through the telegraph services, as a lowly messenger boy. In the late 19th century, messenger boys went by foot, darting between the horse-drawn carriages and the crinolines delicately dodging the mud. Post-Federation, the telegraph boys weaved their way through the cities' early automobiles, bicycle bells clanging. And by the 1930s, the urgent messages the telegraph boys carried were invariably delivered by motorcycle, spluttering their way down country lanes or past neat new rows of California bungalows sprouting up in the cities' modern suburbs.

After devoting several years studying morse telegraphy by night at the Postal Institute, many a diligent telegraph messenger harboured ambitions of becoming somebody important—a telegraphist, one who received and deciphered those vital messages. And surviving morse-codians today still delight in swapping stories of telegraph messenger boy howlers, and errands completed above and beyond the call of duty. There's the one about the telegram boy given a 'please explain' note by his superiors as to why he took so long to deliver a telegram. His reply was that he was only told 'to hurry back' and not to hurry there. And the one about the young lad from Hobart instructed to deliver a telegram addressed to the Local Court Magistrate. Dodging the constable on court duty and ducking various court officials, the boy proudly placed the all-important telegram on the magistrate's table—mid-session. Then there's the one about the telegraph messenger who was dispatched from Sydney's Central Telegraph Office late one night with a telegram for an addressee in a suburb 18 kilometres away. The address led him into the dark, unlit scrub, and door knocking on neighbouring houses failed to reveal his destination. So the lad hoofed it back into town to seek the assistance of the local policeman, who related the problem to the proprietor of the local picture theatre, who in turn duly halted the night's movie to display a message on the giant screen requesting information on the whereabouts of the advertised addressee. A postman in the audience stepped forward, the information was imparted and the telegram delivered according to his directions. The movie resumed.

Doug Mitchell, a former operations supervisor and instructor for Australia Post, started his career as a telegraph boy, rising to telegraph operator in the 1950s. He recalls having only one precisely timed 10-minute toilet break per shift. 'The discipline in the chief telegraph office was very strict,' he recalls. 'You could be a quarter of a minute late for work and you'd still get a paper for being late which you may be fined so many pounds in those days, 5 shillings or 10, whatever, for being late.'

Bendigo Morse Codian Society member Ted Rankins worked as a postwar telegraph operator in small rural Victorian post offices. Grain and fruit prices were standard telegraphic fare, he told the ABC in an interview in August 2007, along with bank telegrams and bank code telegrams. And there were the ubiquitous birthday and wedding telegrams.

'Congratulations and best wishes' was a regular starting point for a telegram, he recalls, which of course would become 'cgs abw'. Long before the days of mobile phones and SMS, telegraphists had invented their own abbreviated language. It was not unheard of for bizarre errors in messages to slip through the system, however, when one too many vowels was omitted. A favourite among morse codians is the startled mother who received a telegram informing her that her son was 'Headed for Russia, hiking through Persia'. She was sure he was hiking in Scotland, travelling through Ross-shire and Perthshire.

Rankins also recalled the pain of being the bearer of sad news, delivering messages of death, sickness and tragic accidents in small, tight-knit communities where everybody knew everybody else.

About the second telegram I delivered was . . . a sympathy telegram for a man I knew, a local man, whose four-year-old daughter had died . . . I met him in his back yard, I delivered the telegram, and he asked me to sit with him for a while and just talk to him. That was fine, but as a 15-year-old boy . . . we weren't counselled or trained in talking with people . . . Because it was a small community and I grew up knowing him, I called him 'mister' all those times . . . and here he was, a grown man, asking me to sit with him and just talk with him. I'll never forget that.

Public service regulations stipulated that only boys aged between 13 and 16 were permitted to be appointed as telegraph messengers. But according to the Australian Heritage Council, there is evidence that before this regulation was brought into force, many young girls also got their first job in the post office working as telegraph messengers. Indeed, the Australian Post Office from its earliest inception offered one of the few employment opportunities for women, and by the 1880s, women were in charge of over half the post offices in Victoria. In rural areas, often these positions were inherited from deceased husbands, as was the case with Jane Miles at the Darlington Post Office, who became Victoria's first unofficial postmistress in 1849. Elsie Barney took over the Moreton Bay Post Office after her husband, Captain James Barney, died in 1855, and when the penal colony became Brisbane, she held on to the position, making her the first woman in the Australian colonies to head a GPO in 1860. In the 1870s, Ellen Kuper at New Norcia Station in Western Australia was promoted from telegraphist to postmistress, earning her the distinction of becoming the first Aboriginal person to hold a senior position in the public service.

Women were also visible at the coalface of mail delivery from the earliest days. Mary Cox took over the twice-weekly 17-hour Hobart to Launceston run when her husband died in 1837, and built up the family business to seven coaches and 150 horses. And for sheer longevity, it would be hard to beat Eliza Jane Morehouse, who began delivering Victoria's Cobden to Camperdown mail six days a week in 1884. In 1923, Morehouse switched from coach to motor car, carefully observing the PMG's rule that the mails should be conveyed at a speed 'not less than six miles an hour [10 kilometres per hour] wherever practicable' during her 14-kilometre journey. She would not retire until 1932, at the respectable age of 90.

The early system worked to the post office's advantage; a female employed in the 19th century could expect to earn as little as half the pay of a man. But the post office did offer respectability, and from the earliest days of the telephone exchanges, women were actively recruited in the belief their innate nurturing qualities made them better suited for dealing with irate customers than their male counterparts.

When the Melbourne metropolitan post office engaged a 16-year-old Catholic schoolgirl from Richmond in 1882, little did it know the move would signal the beginning of a two-decades-long stoush which would ultimately position the Australian Post Office as one of the first equal opportunity employers of the 20th century. Louisa Dunkley, the daughter of an English shoemaker, spent the first six years of her career studying telegraphy, qualifying as an operator in 1888. Two years later, when she was transferred to the Chief Telegraph Office, she became acutely aware of the cavern which separated male and female pay and working conditions.

Dunkley's crusade for equal rights was particularly bruising. While the telegraph and postal unions supported the concept of equal pay and opportunity in virtually all the other colonies, in Victoria the mass sacking of about 1500 mostly male postal employees during the Depression of the 1890s left male unionists in the colony raw and hostile to their female colleagues. In response, Dunkley persuaded her female co-workers to form their own union and in 1900 the Victorian

Women's Post and Telegraph Association made its debut at the all-colonies conference of telegraphists in Sydney. With Federation just around the corner, the conference had been convened to nut out the terms and conditions under which the colonies' post office employees would join a giant Commonwealth public service. Dunkley's articulate and passionate advocacy of equal pay and status under the new Commonwealth was embraced, but not without threats from some furious male delegates that they would fight to have the endorsement reversed. Despite vigorous attacks made in the male union's newspaper, the Victorian Women's Post and Telegraph Association determinedly lobbied Parliament to ensure the *Commonwealth Public Service Act* of 1902 would include provision for equal pay for telegraphists and postmistresses. Dunkley and her union won, and the principle of equal pay has been with us ever since.

In the wake of her 1902 victory, Dunkley married Edward Charles Kraegen. Upon her marriage on 22 December 1903, she resigned her position from the PMG's Department, as was the expectation of the day. Women still had a long way to go.

Some 95 years later, another woman would mark an international milestone for gender equality. In 1997, Australia Post's Linda Nicholls became the first woman in the Western world to serve as chair of a postal authority. Precisely 20 years earlier, Australia Post had endorsed a policy of equal employment opportunity, placing the institution well ahead of government moves to cement such rights in legislation of the 1980s. Increasingly, women made their way into traditionally male-dominated operational areas of the Post Office. Signs of the executive glass ceiling beginning to crack did not appear until 1984, however, with the appointment of Joan Spiller to the position of General Manager of Operations.

In recognition of Dunkley's fighting spirit, a south-east Melbourne federal seat was named after her upon its creation in 1984. It has swung between Liberal and Labor ever since, but remains constant in its feature that the sitting member has always been a man.

⁑

The ghosts of Dunkley, Miles, Barney and Kuper no doubt smile kindly on Valda Knott, who began running the Trayning Post Office in Western Australia when she was just 15 years old. More than 50 years later, she's still there, although her title has changed to licensed postal manager. She admits she never much liked the 'mistress' part of the job description. As well as handling the mail and myriad other postal duties, Knott coordinates the local ambulance service, witnesses documents for the police, serves on the local council, and, when she's taken care of all of that, sees to the town's spiritual needs as the community's minister—wedding, christening and funeral services are the standard ecclesiastical fare. 'The Post Office I think is very important. It is the real hub of the wheel,' she says. 'People meet other people here. They know that everybody in the morning gets their mail so that if they're lonely they can come and sit out the front and know that they will have someone to chat to.'

As a long-term contractor, or 'non-official' post office worker as they were once called, the multi-skilling Knott would empathise with the postmaster of Gundaroo, Ralph Clemenger, who sent a plaintive letter to the New South Wales Deputy Postmaster-General on 10 August 1903:

232

Sir,

In view of the fact that you are empowered to make such arrangements as may be considered desirable with officers who embraced the 'non-official regulation' [a classification of postmaster] framed in August 1896, I respectfully beg to apply for an increase of salary and am hopeful that the following facts will cause my application to receive favourable consideration.

For the past seven years I have received no increase whatever, while officers in charge of surrounding stations of similar status have, during that period, been in receipt of two and in some instances of three increases of salary.

Although regarded as a non-official Post and Telegraph Master, I would like to point out that in every respect I perform similar duties to official officers, and in some matters am actually saddled with work which they are not called upon to undertake. For instance, while several official postmasters who receive the periodical increments have not to perform Electoral duties, and have not to keep their offices open after 6pm, I both act as Deputy Electoral Registrar and do not close until 8pm, being on duty daily from 7.30am to 8.15pm.

The fact that I have been allowed to perform relieving duty at official stations should I think go to prove, that, although I have embraced the non-official regulation, I am hardly viewed in the same light as other non-official officers. I am also called upon to pay the regular fidelity premium, and am expected to perform telegraph messengers duties.

While freely admitting that it was my own desire to embrace the non-official regulation, I feel sanguine that a glance at the papers bearing upon my case will disclose the fact that I was treated with unmerited severity in the initial reorganisation scheme, and that the utter hopelessness of the outlook made me enter into a contract which has been as advantageous to the Department as it has been disastrous to myself.

To find my own Assistant, pay rent for Office premises (which rent has been recently increased), buy my own lights, and give constant and faithful attention for twelve, and often fourteen hours daily, for £120 per annum hardly means a bare existence.

I respectfully contend that the revenue in connection with this office is not a fair indication of the work performed, inasmuch as I handle all the mail matter for several small offices in the locality, such work producing no revenue for which I can take credit. The Departmental book, shewing the interchange of mail between offices, will substantiate what I affirm.

I sincerely trust that you will recommend that I be allowed £145 per annum for my services as non-official Post & Telegraph Master here, and in consideration of my finding my own assistant and office premises.

Should you not be able to accede to my request, perhaps you may see your way clear to allow my wife, Ellen Clemenger (who is a telegraphist and assists me with the work generally) the sum of £26 per annum as temporary assistant.

I may be pardoned for calling attention to the fact that during my lengthy service extending over twenty two years, I have never had a single fine recorded against me for anything whatever.

I have the honor to be Sir,
Your Obedient Servant
W R Clemenger
PM Gundaroo

It remains unknown whether Gundaroo's disgruntled post-master ever received the pay rise he so sorely believed he deserved.

From the tropics of far north Queensland to the post office at the Australian Antarctic Territory base, getting the mail through to some of the most remote corners of the earth, often through drought, bushfires and floods, has been the constant challenge in Australia Post's two centuries of existence. Time has not altered the vast distances travelled by Australia Post's outback posties. At 163,000 square kilometres, the postal network which covers the Broken Hill region of New South Wales is larger than England. The Cape York Peninsula mail area in Far North Queensland is more than twice the size of Victoria. On the edge of the Simpson Desert, weeks are still measured by the postie's visits, just as they were a century earlier by the children of the Never Never. From Port Augusta in South Australia to Birdsville in Queensland and back, the Birdsville Track at 2500 kilometres remains the longest mail run in the world.

More than a century ago, Birdsville was quite the place to be, with a customs office, two pubs, three general stores, a bank and, of course, a post office. Today, Birdsville is part of Australia's outback mythology, an isolated bush town with its population of 100 in winter dropping by half in the searing summer heat that can reach up to 50 degrees. The mail is one way of relieving the isolation. Being a postie isn't a big job, just one delivery a week and maybe a dozen letters for the post office, run by Barrie and Narelle Gaffney, to process. A plane carries the mail between each isolated homestead, with a stretch of six or seven thousand square kilometres separating each stop. But less than half a century ago, the Birdsville Track mail route was still being serviced by land, the mail delivered by an outback legend named Tom Kruse. For almost three decades, Kruse travelled the driest and loneliest road in Australia, weathering sand storms and floods capable of turning the route into a 10-kilometre-wide river which left drowned cattle rotting in the trees and stations submerged for months on end. Mungerannie Station has been washed away twice, and in 1974 Mona Downs was washed away altogether.

Artesian bores sunk at 50-kilometre intervals are the only lifelines in this unforgiving landscape, which has claimed dozens of lives over a century and a half. In 1963, the entire Page Family died on the track after running out of petrol. One of the mail route's first posties, George Roberts, left Birdsville in December 1884 for Haddon Downs. His body was found weeks later.

Esmond Gerald Kruse—known by all as Tom—was just 22 when he took on the Birdsville Track mail route on 1 January 1936. With his Aboriginal assistant Henry Butler, he would make the fortnightly epic journey into the desert in his Leyland Badger for the next 27 years. If everything went to plan, the round trip between Marree and Birdsville would take a week to complete. On one occasion Kruse was missing for six weeks. On one of his first runs a broken tail-shaft forced him to walk in 40-degree heat to Mungerannie and back to Mulka. In 1949, the flooded Cooper Creek saw Kruse co-opting a barge to get the mail through. On another, he got bogged at Pandie Pandie and had to be rescued by plane.

In 1952, Kruse's dedication and determination was captured on film. John Heyer's documentary *Back of Beyond* won the Grand Prix at the Venice International Film Festival in 1954. The following year Kruse was awarded an MBE for 'services to the community in the outback risking his life on many occasions'. He wasn't there to collect the award from the Governor, who had travelled to Birdsville for the presentation. He was stranded on the track somewhere, cut off by floodwaters.

Kruse eventually retired from the mail run in 1963. But to the people who lived along the Birdsville Track, 'there would never be another mailman like Tom'. In October 1999, the 85-year-old Kruse completed the track in his restored Leyland Badger one last time. He delivered more than 7000 letters from all over the world and raised $12,000 for the Royal Flying Doctor Service, before parking his truck permanently at the Birdwood Motor Museum, South Australia.

The stamina and guts of posties such as Kruse and the Fizzer, the heroic feats of Guillaux and Smithy, the sacrifices of a parched gang threading a fragile stretch of wire through thousands of kilometres of harsh rocky desert: a lot has been achieved since Isaac Nichols processed his first mailbag of 36 letters back in 1809. Today, 35,000 Australia Post employees process more than four billion articles a year, in a 24-hour-a-day business. And in any working day some one million customers will stream through the postal network. Be it by plane, truck, bicycle or foot, the mail keeps moving through an ever-evolving process of delivering to a nation.

AUTHOR'S
ACKNOWLEDGEMENTS

Richard Walsh, David Norris, Kerrie Smith and the Royal Flying Doctor Service, Australian Heritage Council, Paolo Totaro, Marcella Hunter, Sam Everingham, Seumas Phelan, Murray Waldron, Australian War Memorial and Ross Gittens

PHOTO CREDITS

Plates 2, 4–7, 10, 11, 14–16, 20 and 24–36: Thanks to Richard Breckon and Elizabeth Gertsakis at Australia Post. Plate 5 by permission of Richard Breckon. Thanks also to Brendan Ward.

Plate 1: Artwork by Iain McKellar.

Plate 3: John Carmichael, 1803–1857, 'Plate no. [2] of: Select views of Sydney, New South Wales' courtesy of the National Library of Australia, Canberra.

Plates 8, 9, 12, 13 and 22: Courtesy of the National Archives of Australia.

Plate 17: Courtesy of the State Library of New South Wales.

Plate 18: Courtesy of the Australian War Memorial, Negative Number E02941.

Plate 19: Thanks to Chris Lloyd for permission to use this photograph.

Plate 21: Photo number PH0200/0177, Mayse Young Collection, courtesy of Northern Territory Library.

Plate 23: Title number 353083, holding 1025. Thanks to the John Heyer Estate for permission to use this photograph, courtesy of the National Film and Sound Archive.

Quotations from the Davis Calwell letters are from the correspondence collection number MS 11492, 1853–1923, held at the State Library of Victoria.

SOURCES

The Stamp of Australia is based on the documentary of the same name, written by Andrew Haughton and Brendan Ward, and draws on interviews conducted for the documentary with the following people:

Nancy Bird-Walton

Dr Mary Elizabeth Calwell

Les Carlyon

Ray Chapman

Dr Elizabeth Farrelly

Barry Gaffney

Dr Bill Gammage

Gideon Haigh

Rex Harcourt

Mark Johnston

Lang Kidby

Valda Knott

Noel Leahy

John May

Dr Ross McMullin

Doug Mitchell

Graeme Nichols

Bernard Salt

Glen Stephens

Bill Storer

Ian Thorpe

Jeff Watson

A select list of sources follows.

Newspapers: *The Age, Sydney Morning Herald, Daily Telegraph, Australian Financial Review, Business Review Weekly*

Aspinal, Clara, *Three years in Melbourne*, London: L. Booth, 1862

Lee, Robert, *Linking a Nation: Australia's Transport and Communications, 1788–1970*, Australian Heritage Commission, online, 2003

Carlyon, Les, *Gallipoli*, Pan Macmillan Australia, 2002

——, *The Great War*, Pan Macmillan Australia, 2006

Everingham, Sam, *Wild ride: The rise and fall of Cobb & Co*, Camberwell, Vic: Penguin Group (Australia), 2007

BIBLIOGRAPHY

Fysh, Hudson, *Qantas Rising*, Longreach, Qld: Qantas Founders Outback Museum, 1996

Gibbs, Stephen, 'The frail judge, his stamps and the carer who tried to sell them', *Sydney Morning Herald*, 15 September 2004

Gammage, Bill, *The Broken Years: Australian soldiers in the Great War*, Ringwood, Vic: Penguin Books, 1990

Gunn, Jeannie, *We of the Never-Never*, Hutchinson, 1983

Hunter, Marcella, *Australia Post: Delivering more than ever*, Edgecliff, NSW: Focus Publishing, 2000

The Inlander: A quarterly magazine dealing with national interests from the outbacker's point of view, Sydney: Home Mission Board of the Presbyterian Church of Australia, 1913–1951

McHugh, Siobhan, *The Snowy: The people behind the power*, Pymble, NSW: Angus & Robertson, 1995

Nicholas, Stephen and Peter R. Shergold, 'Transportation as Global Migration', in S. Nicholas, (ed.) *Convict Workers: Reinterpreting Australia's Past*, Cambridge: Cambridge University Press, 1988

Onward Speed, dir. Fred Schepisi, corporate film, The Film House, National Film and Sound Archive

Peel, Mark, et al., *Stamping the Nation: Australia since Federation*, Melbourne: Australia Post, 2001

Penglase, Joanna and David Horner, *When the War Came to Australia: Memories of the Second World War*, St Leonards, NSW: Allen & Unwin, 1992

Tench, Watkin, *A narrative of the expedition to Botany-Bay*, [electronic resource], eBooks@Adelaide, The University of Adelaide Library, University of Adelaide, SA, 2006

INDEX